Nǐ Hǎo

Student Workbook
Introductory Level

(Traditional character edition)

正 體 字 版

by

Shumang Fredlein ● Paul Fredlein

Cheng & Tsui Company, Boston

Nǐ Hǎo 1 – Student Workbook
Introductory level
(Traditional character edition)

The traditional character edition of Ni Hao 1 was published by ChinaSoft in 1995 and a North American edition was published by Cheng & Tsui in 2001

This revised North American edition was published in 2003 by
Cheng & Tsui Company
25 West Street
Boston, MA 02111-1213 USA
Fax (617) 426-3669
www.cheng-tsui.com
"Bringing Asia to the World"™
by arrangement with ChinaSoft Pty Ltd, Australia
Web: http://www.chinasoft.com.au

Written by Shumang Fredlein (林淑滿) & Paul Fredlein
Illustrated by Xiaolin Xue (薛曉林), Zhengdong Su (蘇正東), Bo wu (吳波), Jemma Fredlein
Edited by Sitong Jan (詹絲桐)
Typeset by ChinaSoft on Apple Macintosh

Textbook, audio cassettes and CD-ROMs are also available.

ISBN-10: 0-88727-415-3
ISBN-13: 978-0-88727-415-2

15 14 13 12 11 10 9 8 7

Printed in the United States of America

Foreword

The *Ni Hao 1 Student Workbook* is a learning activity book based on the content introduced in the *Ni Hao 1 Textbook – Chinese Language Course, Introductory Level*. This workbook contains a variety of activities that provide opportunities for students to practice the four communication skills – listening, speaking, reading and writing. Activities can be adapted to suit students' needs and abilities, e.g. the listening exercises can be used for speaking; the reading and writing exercises can also be used for listening and speaking.

The listening exercises for each lesson are included in the Teacher's Handbook and recorded on audio cassettes/CDs. The teacher may play the tape/CDs to the class, or alternatively, read out the passages from the Teacher's Handbook. Answers to all the questions in this book are included in the Teacher's Handbook.

Chinese characters are used in conjunction with Pinyin to reinforce reading and writing skills. Students are not required to write exclusively in characters, but are encouraged to use a combination of Pinyin and characters. The Textbook lists characters students should learn to write. These characters are also included in the *Writing Exercise* and *Character Bricks* sections of this book. Students should always write characters in the correct stroke order and in good proportion. This provides the foundation for beautiful handwriting which is always appreciated by Chinese.

* * * *

Many thanks are owed to Mrs Juanita Yuen who provided us with her teaching materials and to many others for valuable advice and suggestions.

Contents

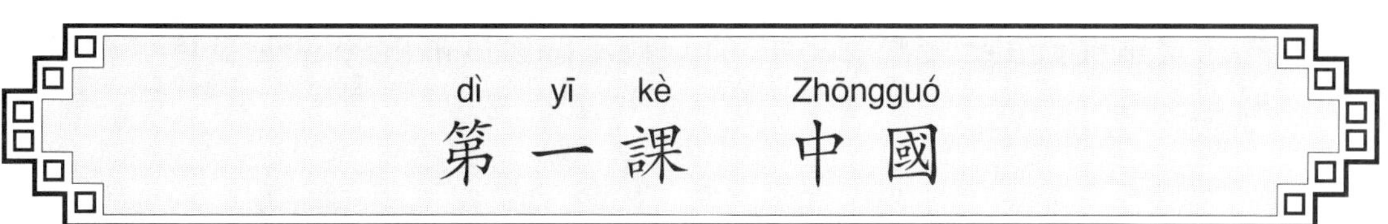

A Do research on China and complete the following sentences.

1. China, in Chinese, is called Zhōngguó (中國), which means ___Middle country___.

2. The Chinese national language, known in English as Mandarin, is called Pǔtōnghuà (普通話), which means ___Common tongue___. It is also called Hànyǔ (漢語), which comes from the name of the majority race called the ___han___ people.

3. Mandarin is used as the official language by three countries/areas. They are China, ___Taiwan___ and ___Singapore___.

4. The population of China is ___1.3 Billion___, which is about ___4___ times that of the United States.

5. The area of China is ___3,696,100___ mile^2, which is about ___1___ times that of the United States.

6. The capital of China is ___Beijing___.

7. The most famous animal native to China is ___the Panda___.

8. The only man-made object visible from outer space is ___the great wall of China___.

9. The two main rivers in China are ___the Yangtze river___ and ___the yellow river___.

10. The entombed terracotta warriors were found in the city of ___Shaanxi___, and they were built in the reign of Emperor ___Qin Shi Huang___.

B The names of major cities and rivers in China are hidden in the puzzle below. Find and circle them.

H	A	U	N	G	C	C	E	R	S	E	C	K	S
H	U	A	N	G	H	E	B	A	H	A	D	D	S
S	U	G	A	R	A	R	E	N	A	T	H	U	S
H	A	R	B	I	N	B	I	I	N	O	O	N	E
E	A	S	Y	I	G	I	J	I	G	O	H	H	T
N	O	S	E	S	J	H	I	I	H	H	U	U	T
Y	E	S	A	X	I	A	N	O	A	H	S	A	S
A	R	E	N	N	A	U	G	U	I	L	I	N	U
N	O	I	S	A	N	D	W	I	C	H	S	G	Z
G	G	U	A	N	G	Z	H	O	U	G	H	T	H
E	G	G	S	J	E	M	M	A	S	D	A	D	O
G	O	N	E	I	N	H	A	N	G	Z	H	O	U
S	T	I	A	N	J	I	N	S	I	D	E	S	E
C	H	O	N	G	Q	I	N	G	O	I	N	G	S

黄河 Huang He　　長江 Chang Jiang　　西安 Xi'an

廣州 Guangzhou　　北京 Beijing　　哈爾濱 Harbin

瀋陽 Shenyang　　上海 Shanghai　　南京 Nanjing

重慶 Chongqing　　天津 Tianjin　　桂林 Guilin

敦煌 Dunhuang　　蘇州 Suzhou　　杭州 Hangzhou

C Refer to the cities numbered on the map and list them in Pinyin with their important features.

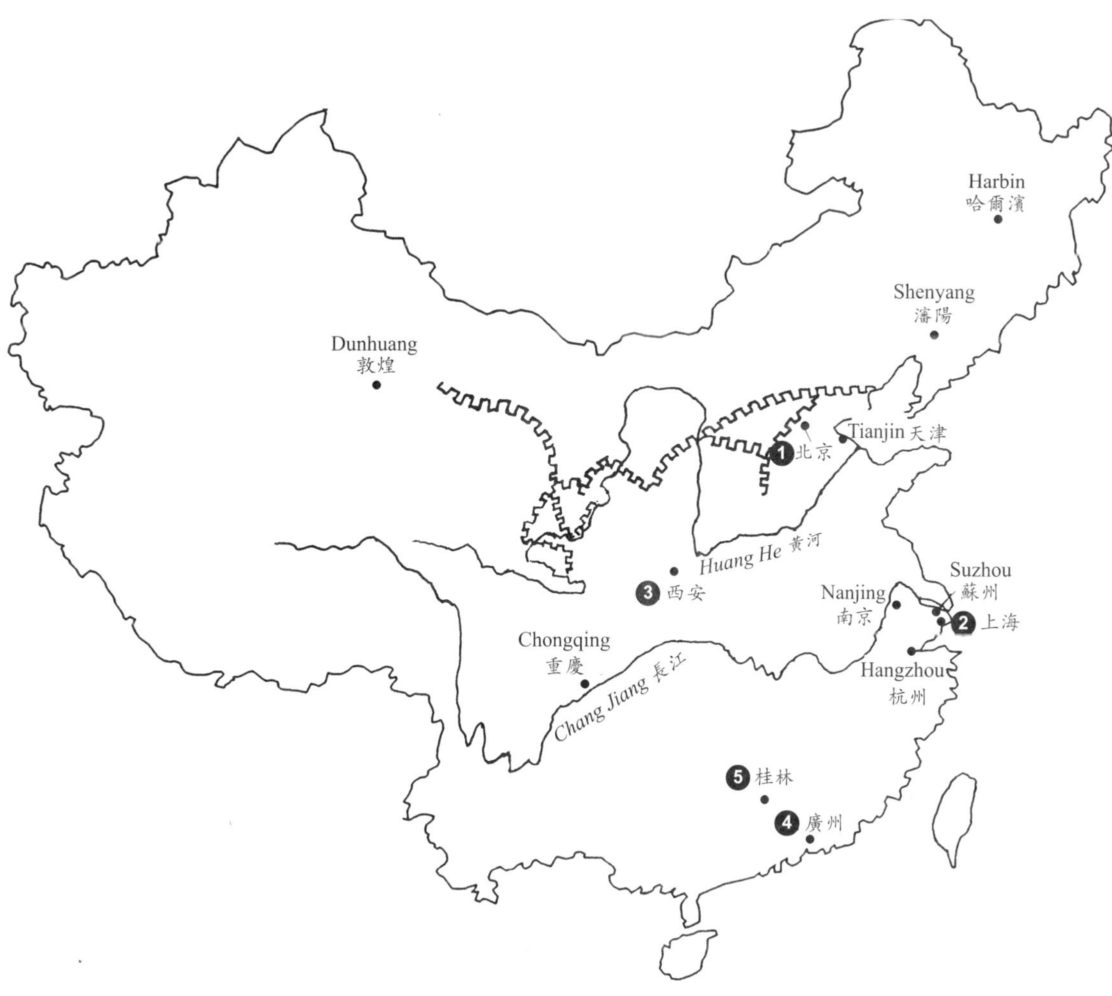

Pinyin: Features:

1. ______________________ ____

2. ______________________ ____

3. ______________________ ____

4. ______________________ ____

5. ______________________ ____

D What do you know about the Chinese language? Choose the appropriate answer for each question. There may be more than one correct answer for some questions.

1. [ ] What is the official language of China?

   (a) Cantonese **(b)** Taiwanese **(c)** Mandarin

2. [ ] The basis of the Chinese writing system is

   (a) alphabetical **(b)** pictographic **(c)** tonal.

3. [ ] The earliest Chinese writings discovered

   (a) were written over 3,000 years ago **(b)** were inscribed on oracle bones

   (c) were inscribed on turtle shells.

4. [ ] Each Chinese character is pronounced as

   (a) one syllable **(b)** two syllables **(c)** various syllables.

5. [ ] The style of Chinese writing currently used is

   (a) simplified **(b)** traditional **(c)** neither.

6. [ ] The official style of Chinese writing in China is

   (a) simplified **(b)** traditional **(c)** both.

7. [ ] The traditional style of writing is currently used in

   (a) China **(b)** Taiwan **(c)** overseas Chinese communities.

8. [ ] The method of writing a Chinese character is

   (a) left to right **(b)** top to bottom **(c)** a tick and a hook.

9. [ ] The pronunciation system currently used in China is

   (a) Wade-Giles system **(b)** International system **(c)** Pinyin.

10. [ ] Apart from the neutral tone, how many tones are there in spoken Chinese?

    (a) four tones **(b)** two tones **(c)** numerous tones.

E Listen to the tape/CD and choose the correct answer (a, b, c).

	a	b	c
1. ______	a. dào	b. diào	c. dài
2. ______	a. páng	b. pán	c. pián
3. ______	a. bāi	b. pāi	c. bāo
4. ______	a. ná	b. nú	c. nuó
5. ______	a. huǎng	b. fǎng	c. lǎng
6. ______	a. mèn	b. fèn	c. rèn
7. ______	a. zhāng	b. chāng	c. shāng
8. ______	a. cài	b. zài	c. sài
9. ______	a. rǎo	b. shǎo	c. zhǎo
10. ______	a. guāi	b. gāi	c. gāo
11. ______	a. jiā	b. xiā	c. qiā
12. ______	a. wǎn	b. yuǎn	c. huǎn
13. ______	a. xuān	b. suān	c. quān
14. ______	a. shì	b. sì	c. rì
15. ______	a. yòng	b. xiōng	c. róng
16. ______	a. rǎng	b. shàng	c. cáng
17. ______	a. xué	b. xiē	c. shuǐ
18. ______	a. lù	b. lǜ	c. luè
19. ______	a. liú	b. liào	c. luó
20. ______	a. zǐ	b. sī	c. cì

F Listen to the tape/CD and choose the correct answer (a, b, c, d).

	a	b	c	d
1. ______	a. yū	b. yú	c. yǔ	d. yù
2. ______	a. yuē	b. yué	c. yuě	d. yuè
3. ______	a. māo	b. máo	c. mǎo	d. mào
4. ______	a. niāo	b. niáo	c. niǎo	d. niào
5. ______	a. gōu	b. góu	c. gǒu	d. gòu

G You have learned that many Chinese characters were originally drawings of the objects they represent. The earlier the style of character, the closer the character resembles the object.

You will be given three sets of cards. The red set has the modern characters, the blue set has the old style of writing and the yellow set has pictures of the actual objects. Use the blue cards as the bridge between the yellow set and the red set to match the three sets of cards. You will then be able to discover the meaning of the characters for yourself.

Character	Old writing	Meaning	Character	Old writing	Meaning
rì 日	________	________	nǚ 女	________	________
yuè 月	________	________	zǐ 子	________	________
shān 山	________	________	rén 人	________	________
shuǐ 水	________	________	mén 門	________	________
huǒ 火	________	________	chē 車	________	________
kǒu 口	________	________	shǔ 鼠	________	________
shǒu 手	________	________	tù 兔	________	________
ěr 耳	________	________	yáng 羊	________	________
mù 木	________	________	mǎ 馬	________	________

H Circle the character that matches the picture in each frame.

山 日 	羊 馬 	火 月 	山 人 
車 馬 	山 火 	水 火 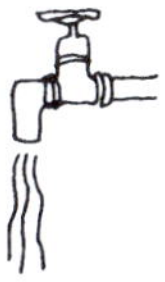	馬 月 
羊 兔 	女 門 	兔 子 	山 門 
口 子 	山 手 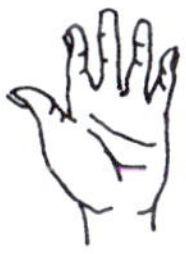	火 木 	口 日 
鼠 耳 	人 水 	口 山 	羊 耳 

I The numbers indicate the stroke order of the Chinese characters. Color each stroke according to the color indicated.

1 — red　　2 — orange　　3 — yellow

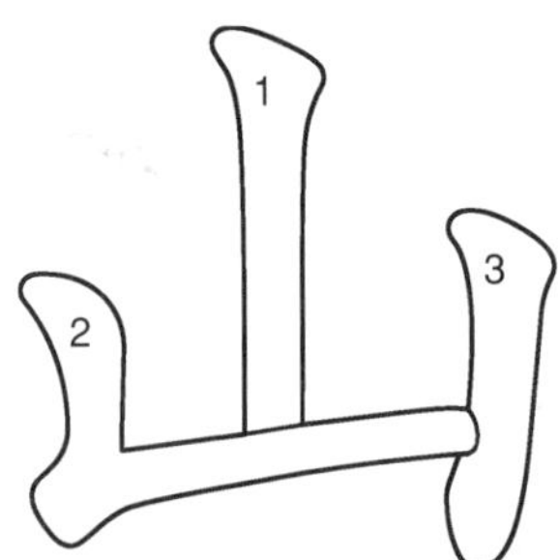

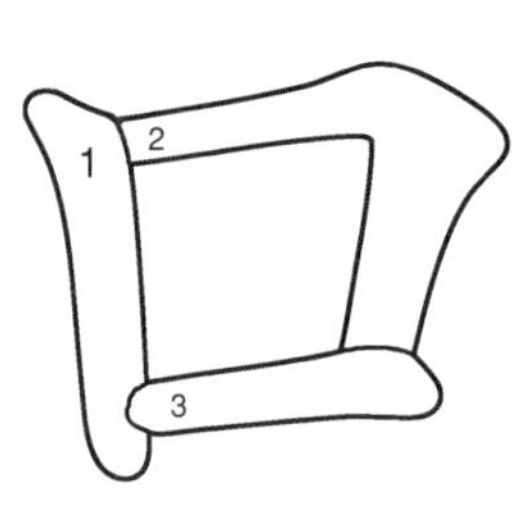

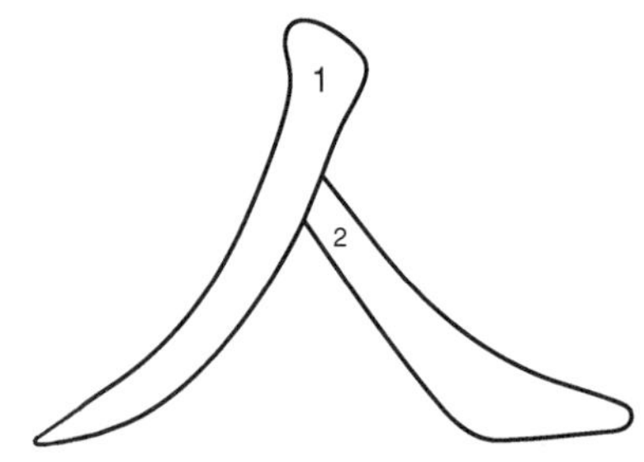

J Guess the meaning of the following combined characters.

1. 山水 ____________　　2. 火車 ____________

3. 口水 ____________　　4. 人口 ____________

5. 水車 ____________　　6. 火山 ____________

K Write in each box the Chinese character which matches the picture.

dì èr kè nǐ hǎo
第二課 你好

A Listen to the statement and choose the best answer.

1. [ ] a  b  c

2. [ ] a  b  c

3. [ ] a  b  c

4. [ ] a  b  c

5. [ ] a  b  c

6. [ ] a  b  c

B This is your first meeting with 蘭蘭 Lánlán. Draw yourself in the oval on the right and write your part of the conversation.

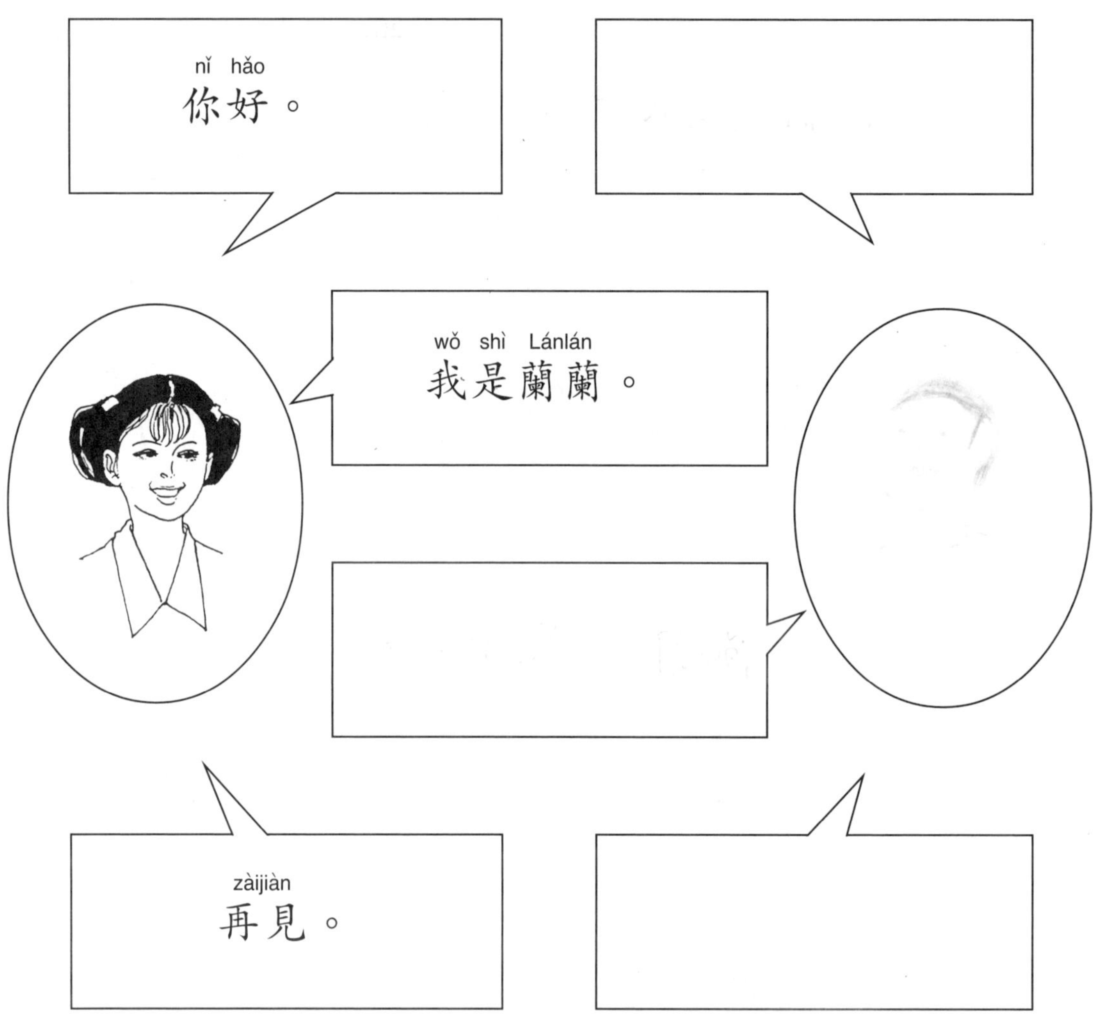

C Now that you can recognize some Chinese words, write the meaning of the following.

1. 再見 ______________
2. 你好 ______________
3. 老師好 ______________
4. 早 ______________
5. 同學們好 ______________
6. 老師再見 ______________

D This is a list of some famous Chinese people. Write their last names and first names in the spaces. Then briefly research and report on each person.

1. Máo Zédōng 毛澤東 last name ____________ first name ____________

   information ____

2. Sūn Yìxiān 孫逸仙 last name ____________ first name ____________

   information ____

3. Dèng Xiǎopíng 鄧小平 last name ____________ first name ____________

   information ____

4. Jiǎng Jièshí 蔣介石 last name ____________ first name ____________

   information ____

5. Jiāng Qīng 江青 last name ____________ first name ____________

   information ____

6. Qū Yuán 屈原 last name ____________ first name ____________

   information ____

E Choose the correct conversation for each of the situations given below and write the answer in the box provided.

zàijiàn 再見。	你好。	tóngxué 同學們好。
lǎoshī 老師好。	zǎo 早。	

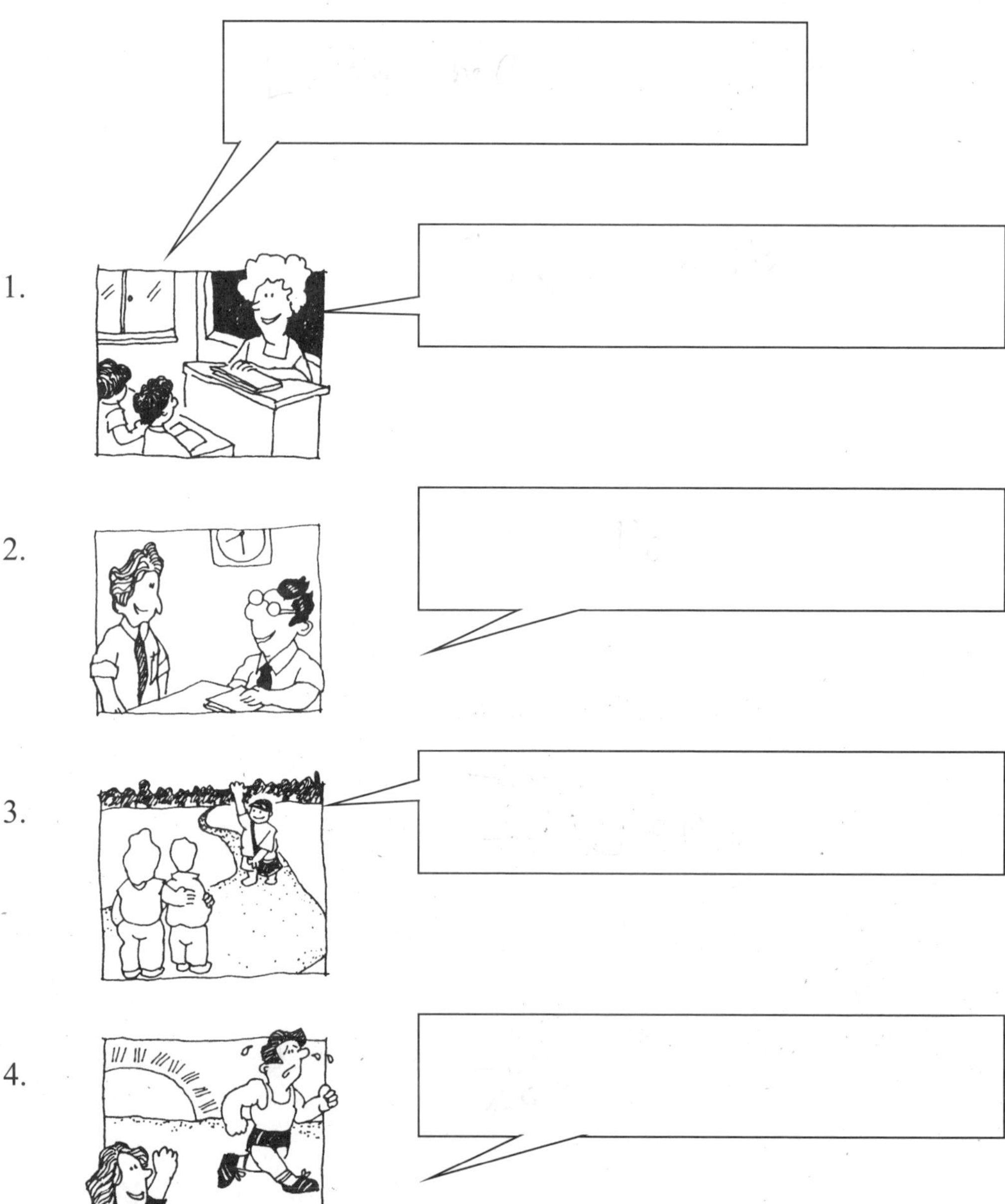
1.
2.
3.
4.

F Write appropriate answers in the blanks to complete the following sentences.

1. The most common way Chinese greet each other is to say ____________________ .

2. The character 好 (good) is a combination of 女, meaning __________ , and 子, meaning __________ .

3. The reason for combining 女 and 子 to mean good is____ .

4. In English, am is used for "I", are for "you" and is for "he" and "she". In Chinese, the single word __________ is used for all of the above.

5. There is a common element in the characters 你, 他 and 們, which is __________ , meaning ____________________ .

6. The plural word for a pronoun or a noun associated with people is .

7. The plural form of 你 is __________ , of 我 is __________ , of 他 is __________ and of 她 is __________ .

8. In a Chinese name the order of the first name and family name is______________________________ .

9. Instead of using Mr. or Mrs., Chinese students address their teachers as __________ .

10. Assume your Chinese teacher's last name is 白, you should call your teacher _____ .

dì sān kè　yī èr sān

第三課　一二三

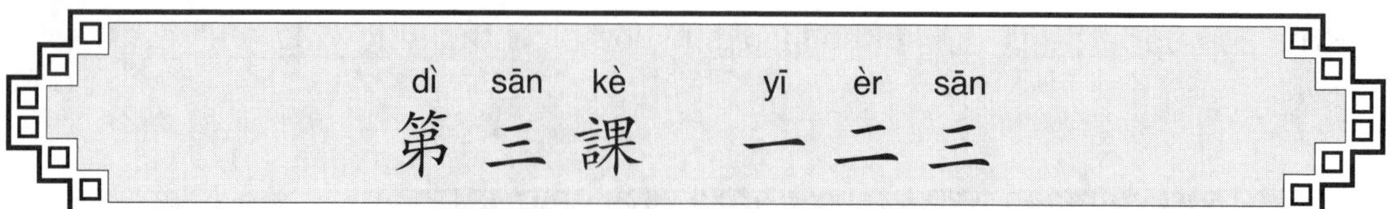

A What is in the picture? Color in the picture according to the colors indicated by the numbers to discover the answer.

1 - green　2 - orange　3 - red　4 - white　5 - black

6 - yellow　7 - purple　8 - brown　9 - light blue

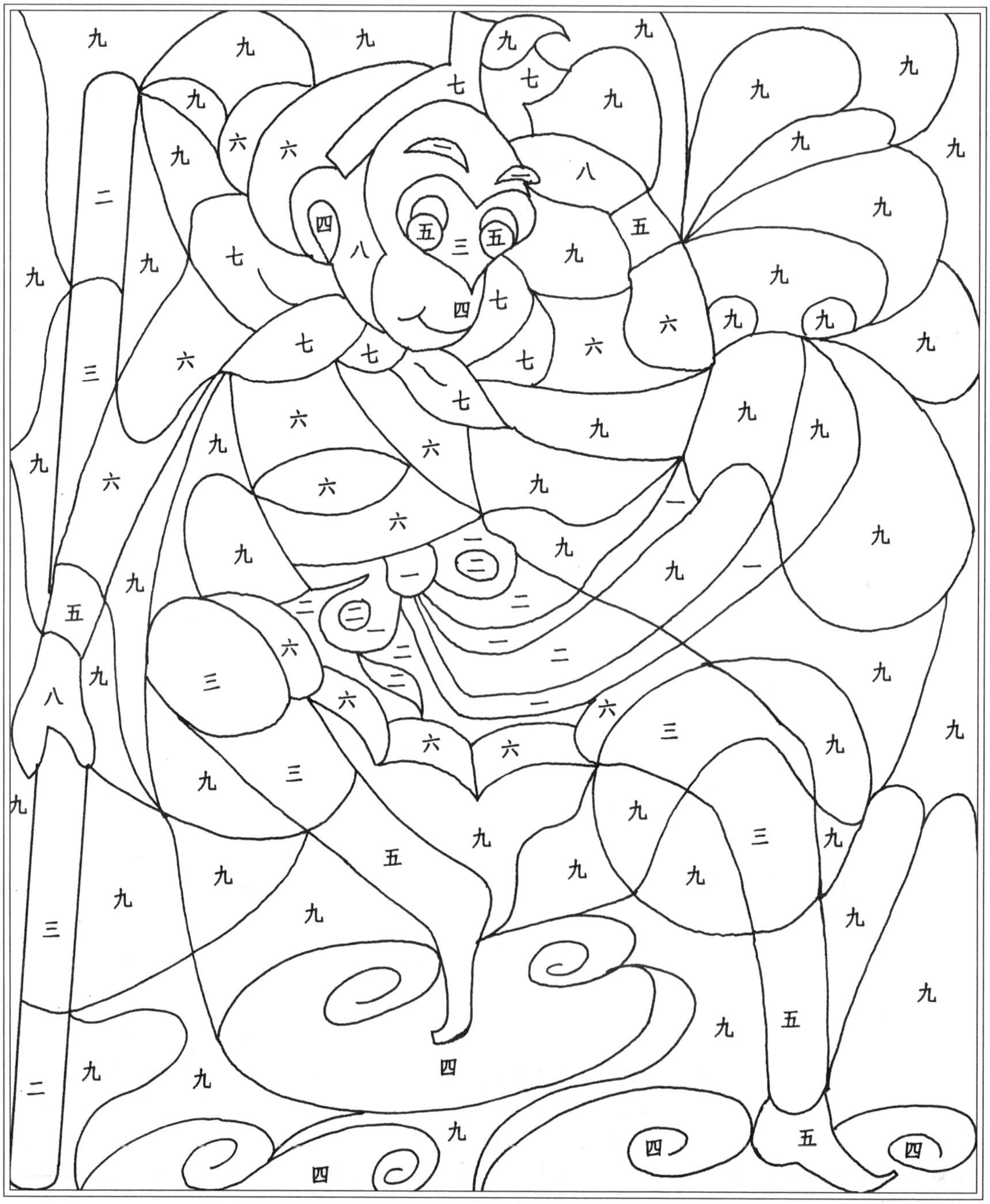

B Draw a line from the Chinese character to the correct match.

1. (a) 五 九 六 一 三

   (b) 9 6 3 5 1

2. (a) 八 七 〇 一 四

   (b) 7 4 1 0 8

3. (a) 二 六 四 八 三

   (b) bā sì èr sān liù

4. (a) 十 五 六 〇

   (b) wǔ liù shí líng yī

C Here are five telephone numbers. Rewrite the Chinese numbers in English and the English numbers in Chinese.

1. 六 八 五 二 九 七 二 Tel: ____________________

2. 四 五 八 九 七 六 三 Tel: ____________________

3. 三 八 一 七 四 三 六 Tel: ____________________

4. 1542109 Tel: ________________________________

5. 7810563 Tel: ________________________________

D Write two of your important telephone numbers and recite them to the class.

	English	Chinese
1.	____________________	______________________________
2.	____________________	______________________________

E Count the objects in each frame and write the answer in Chinese.

F Now write the numbers 1-10 in ascending order.

______ ______ ______ ______ ______ ______ ______ ______ ______ ______

G What is the picture? Join the numbered dots to find out, then color it in.

H 孫悟空 Sūn Wùkōng, the monkey king, is half-way on his journey to the Jade Temple. Write the number of each cloud he rides.

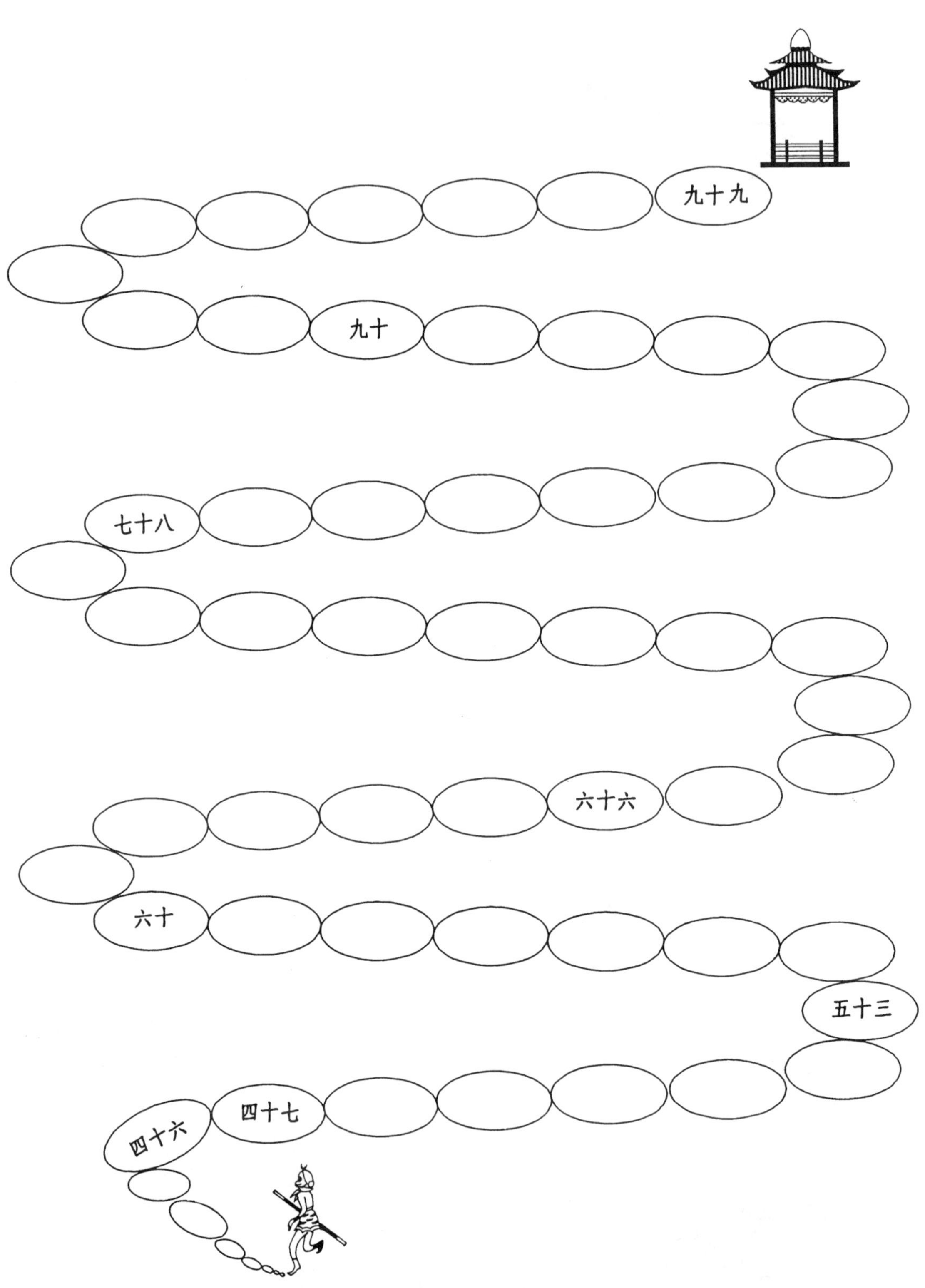

I The numbers are jumbled, rewrite them in ascending order.

1. 八十，七十，四十，九十，六十，五十

2. 十二，二十，八，八十，八十八，五十九

3. 六十三，三，十九，二十五，八，四十七

4. 二十，三十五，二十五，十五，三十，四十

5. 九，一，七十一，二十八，三十四，十七

J These are boxes for you to play bingo or tick-tack-toe.

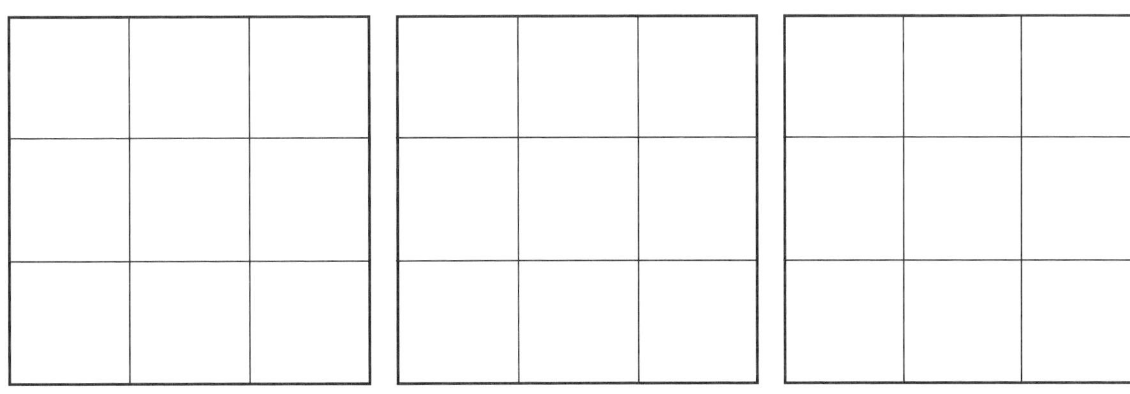

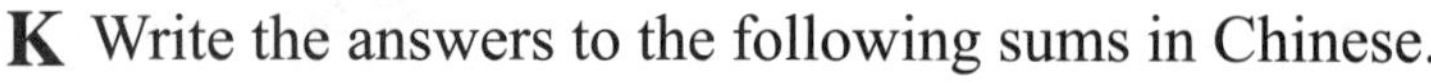

K Write the answers to the following sums in Chinese.

1. 八加(jiā)五等於(děngyú) ＿＿＿＿＿＿。

2. 二十六加(jiā)三十七等於(děngyú) ＿＿＿＿＿＿。

3. 十三減(jiǎn)四等於(děngyú) ＿＿＿＿＿＿。

4. 八十三減(jiǎn)六十二等於 ＿＿＿＿＿＿。

5. 九加六減七等於 ＿＿＿＿＿＿。

6. 七減二加十等於 ＿＿＿＿＿＿。

7. 四乘以(chéng yǐ)六等於 ＿＿＿＿＿＿。

8. 九乘以(chéng yǐ)七等於 ＿＿＿＿＿＿。

9. 十八除(chú)以三等於 ＿＿＿＿＿＿。

10. 四十二除(chú)以六等於 ＿＿＿＿＿＿。

11. 二十四除以六，乘以三等於 ＿＿＿＿＿＿。

12. 四加二減三，乘以八，除以六，加一等於 ＿＿＿＿＿＿。

L Solve the following puzzle by filling in all the blanks in Chinese.

三	+	十二	=		−	一
+		x		÷		x
二十一	−		=	二	+	
+		÷		x		+
	÷	六	=	三	x	
−		+		+		−
三十四	−		=	二十五	+	二
=		=		=		=
	−	十一	=		+	二十

dì sì kè　tā shì shéi
第四課　他是誰

A Listen to the statement and choose the best answer.

1. [　　　] 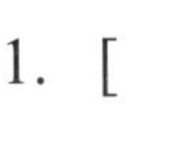 
a. 

b. 

c. 

2. [　　　] 
a. 

b. 

c. 

3. [　　　] 
a. 

b. 

c. 

4. [　　　] 
a. 

b. 

c. 

5. [　　　] 
a. 

b. 

c. 

6. [　　　]  
a. 

b. 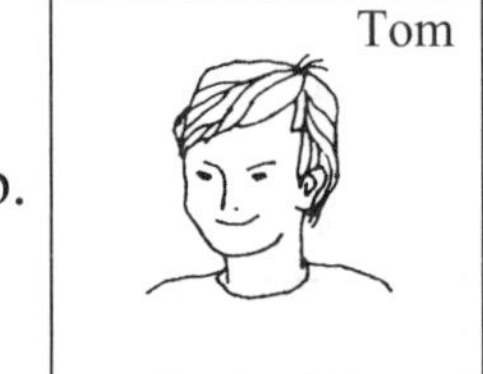

c. 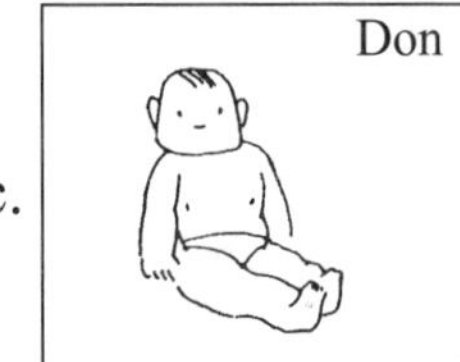

7. [　　] a. She is seventy years old.
b. Mary is seventeen years old.
c. She is Mary.

8. [　　] a. I am ten years old this year.
b. You are ten years old.
c. I am four years old.

9. [　　] a. How old is he?
b. How old are you this year?
c. Who is she?

10. [　　] a. How old is he this year?
b. How old are you?
c. Who is he?

B These are pictures of Don from childhood to old age. Select and write the age that matches the picture.

九十二歲，	一歲，	十四歲，
五十六歲，	三歲	

__________ __________ __________ __________ __________

C Draw yourself in the blank box, then complete the conversation by asking or answering the question where required.

1. 他是誰？

____________________。

2. 她是誰？

____________________。

3. ______________？

他是Ben。

4. 他幾歲？

他 ______________歲。

5. ______________？

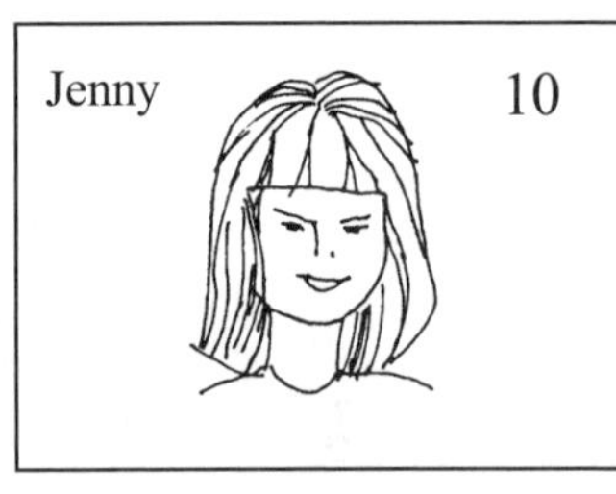

她十歲。

6. 你幾歲？

____________________。

D Draw pictures of your family, your pets or your friends in the circles on the left and write sentences, in Chinese, stating their names and ages.

他是大偉(Dàwěi)。

他十一歲。

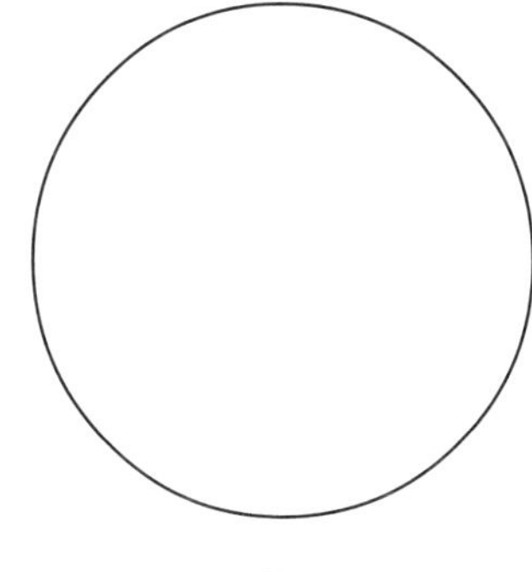

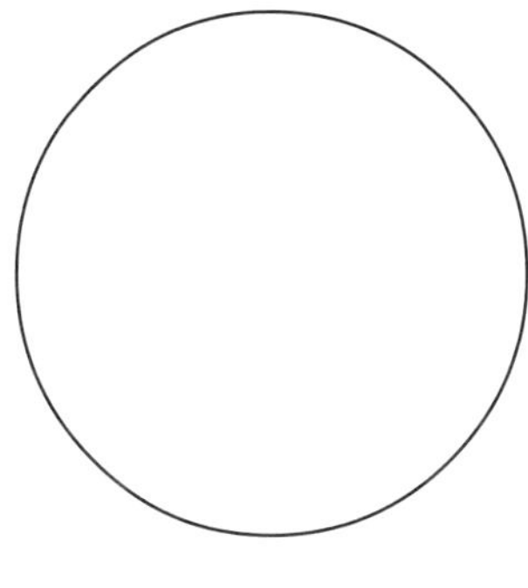

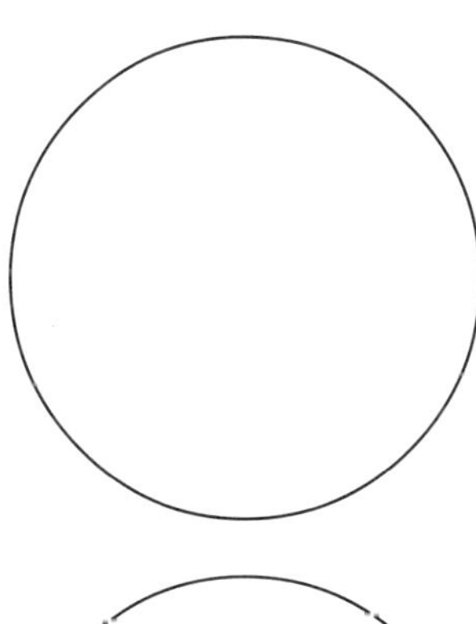

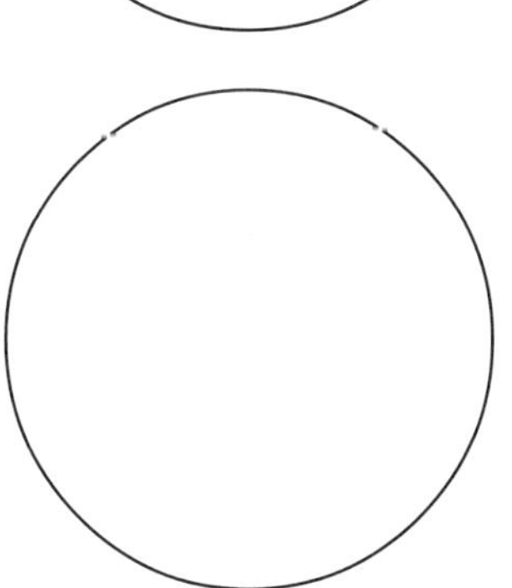

E You stumble onto a web site. This is the message that pops up on the screen. Read the message and answer the questions.

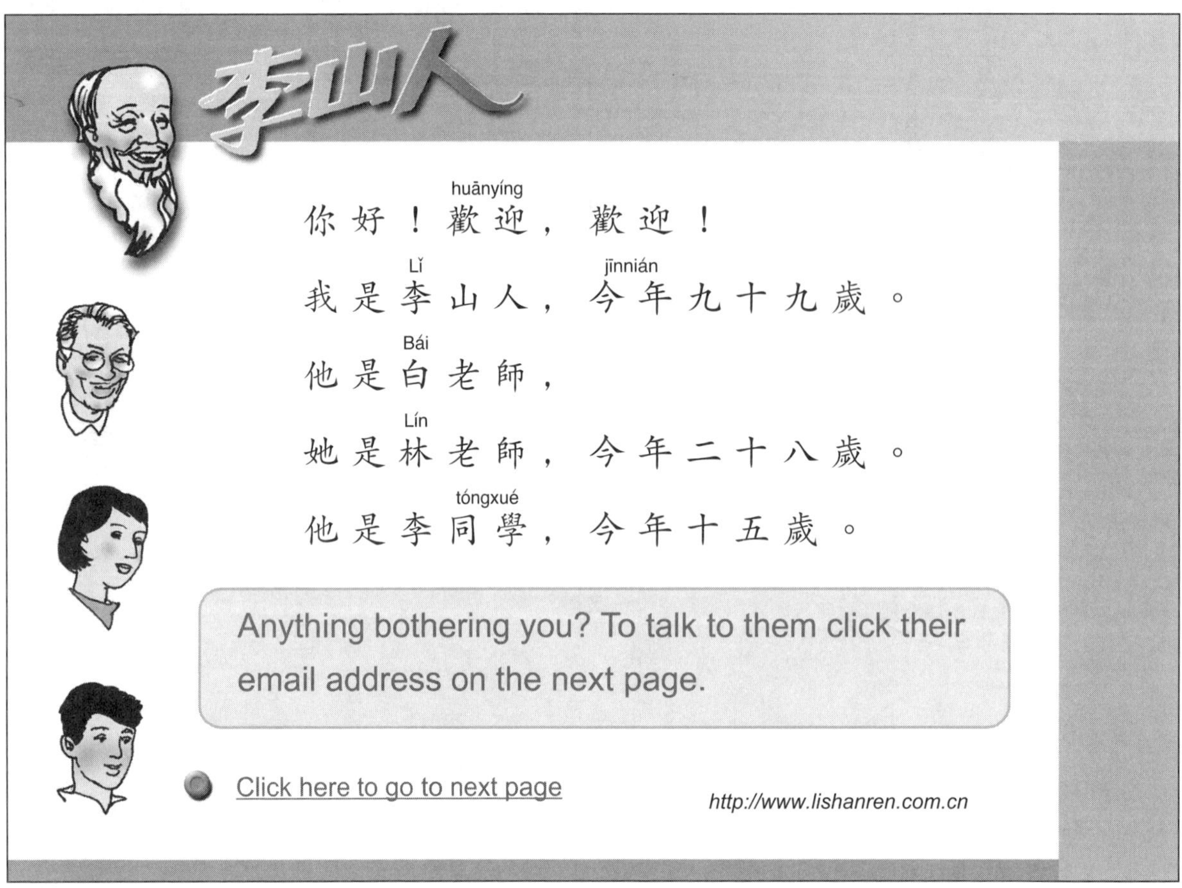

1. Do you think this is a friendly web site? Give evidence to support your answer.

2. Who are these people? State their occupations and ages.

3. Who is the most likely person you would want to talk to? Why?

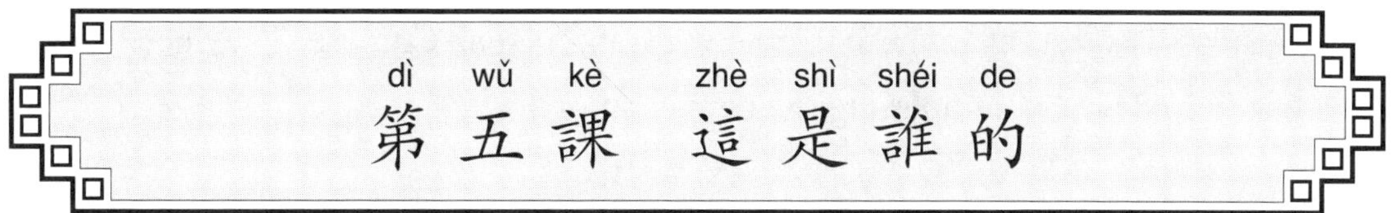

dì wǔ kè zhè shì shéi de
第 五 課　這 是 誰 的

A These are some things used in the classroom. Listen to the tape and choose the correct answer.

1. [　　　] a

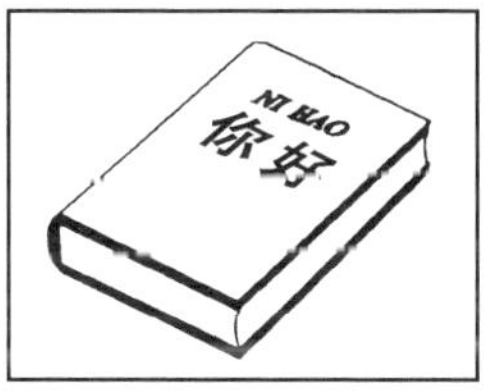

b c

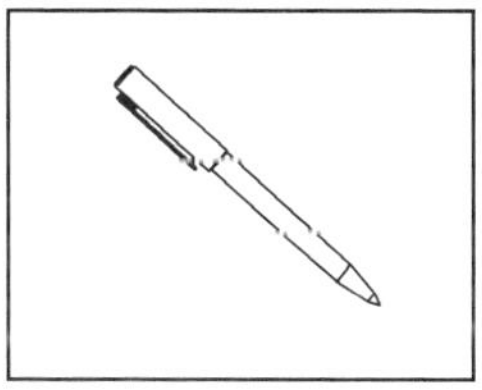

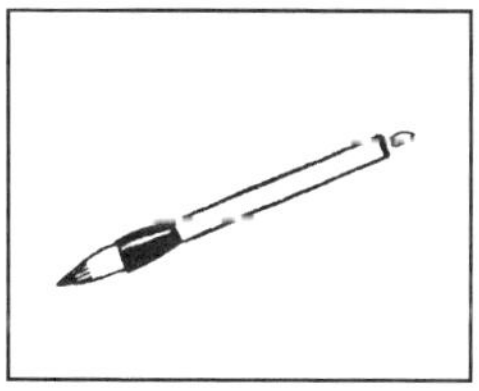

2. [　　　] a b c

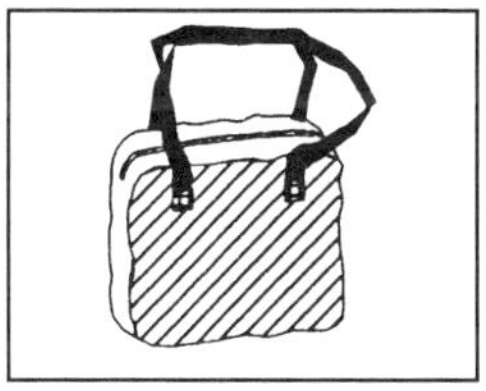

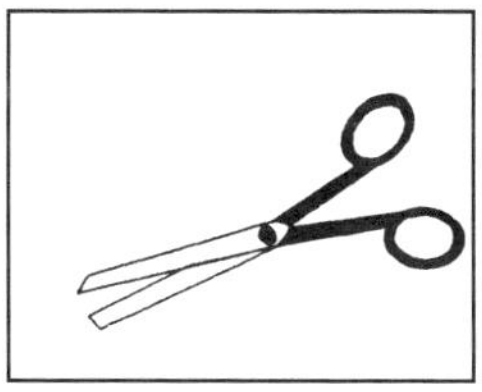

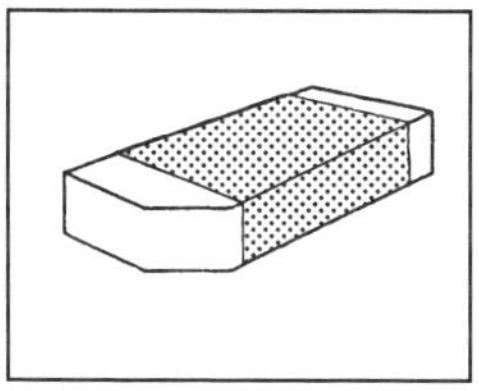

3. [　　　] a b

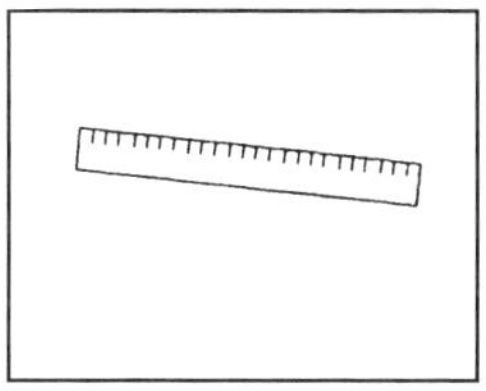

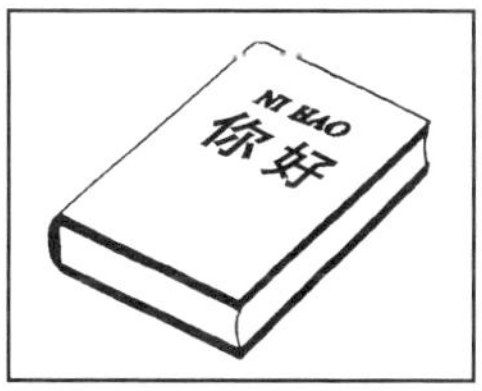

c

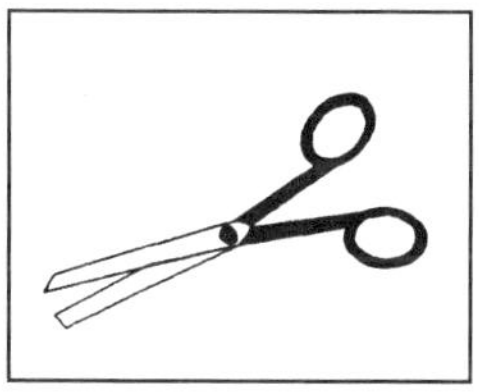

4. [　　　] a b c

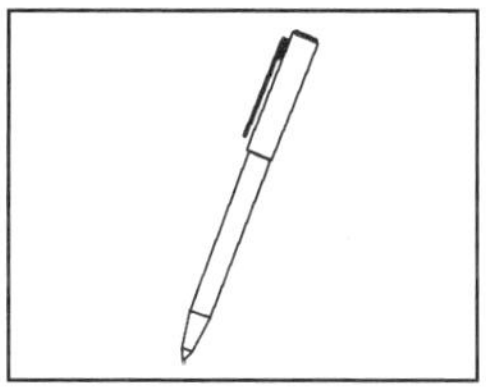

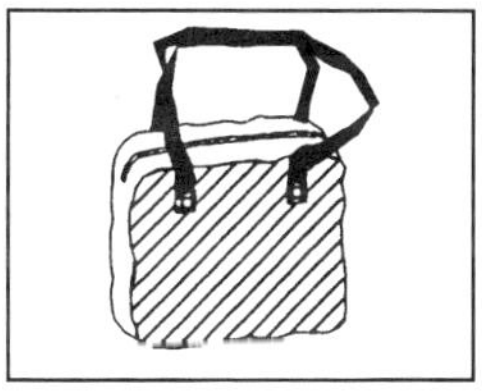

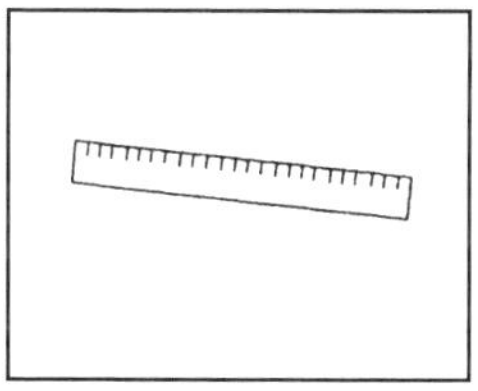

5. [　　　] a

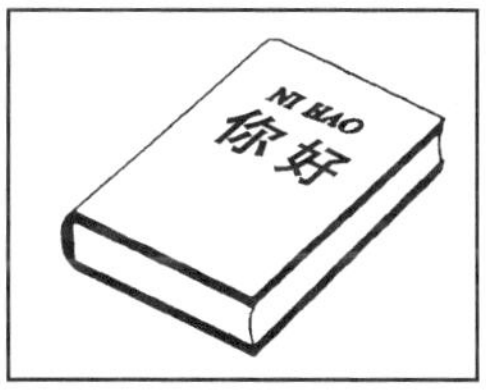

b c

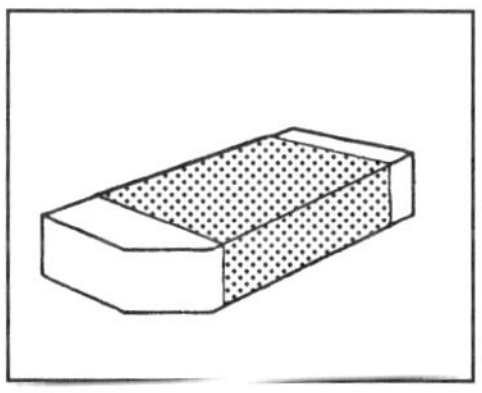

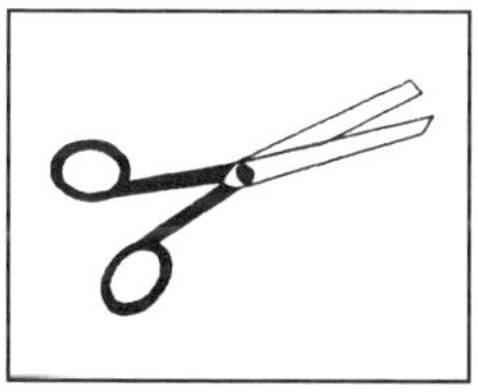

B Draw lines connecting the picture with the matching Chinese word.

xiàngpí 橡皮	jiǎndāo 剪刀	máobǐ 毛筆	bǐ 筆	shū 書	shūbāo 書包

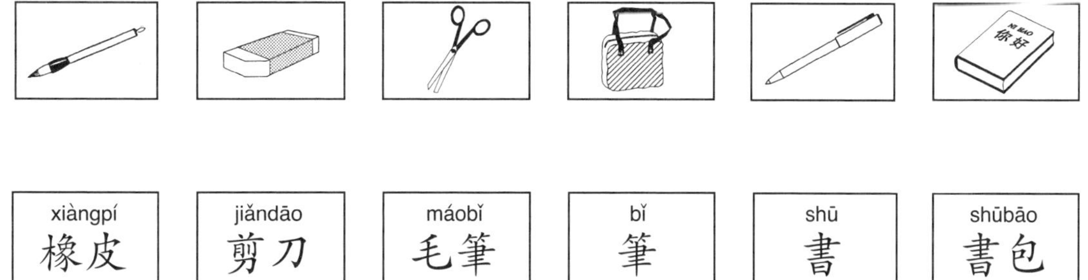

C 蘭蘭 Lánlán is speaking to these people who don't speak Chinese. They need your help! You can help them by completing the conversation.

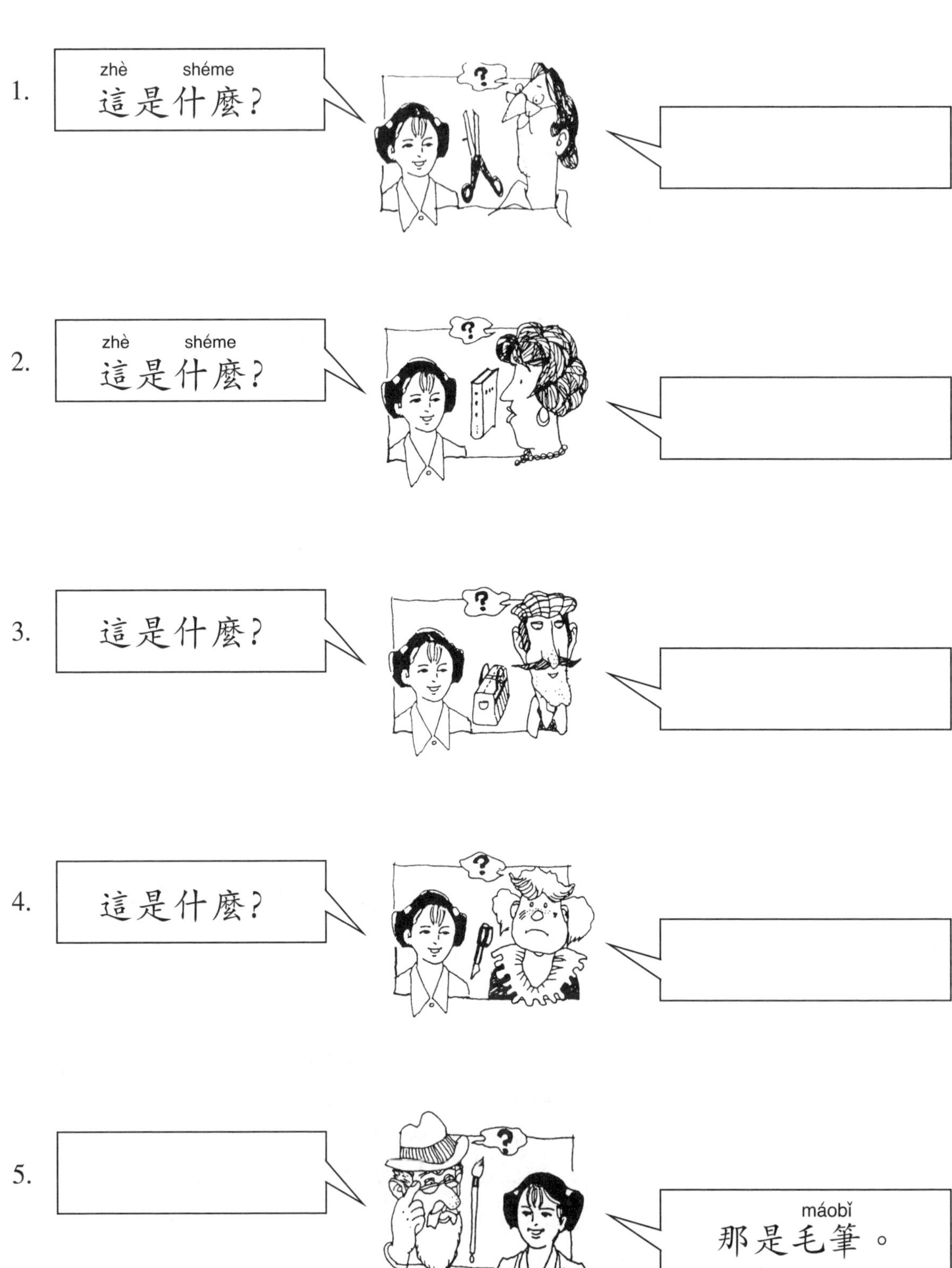

D Discover who owns each object and write your answers below.

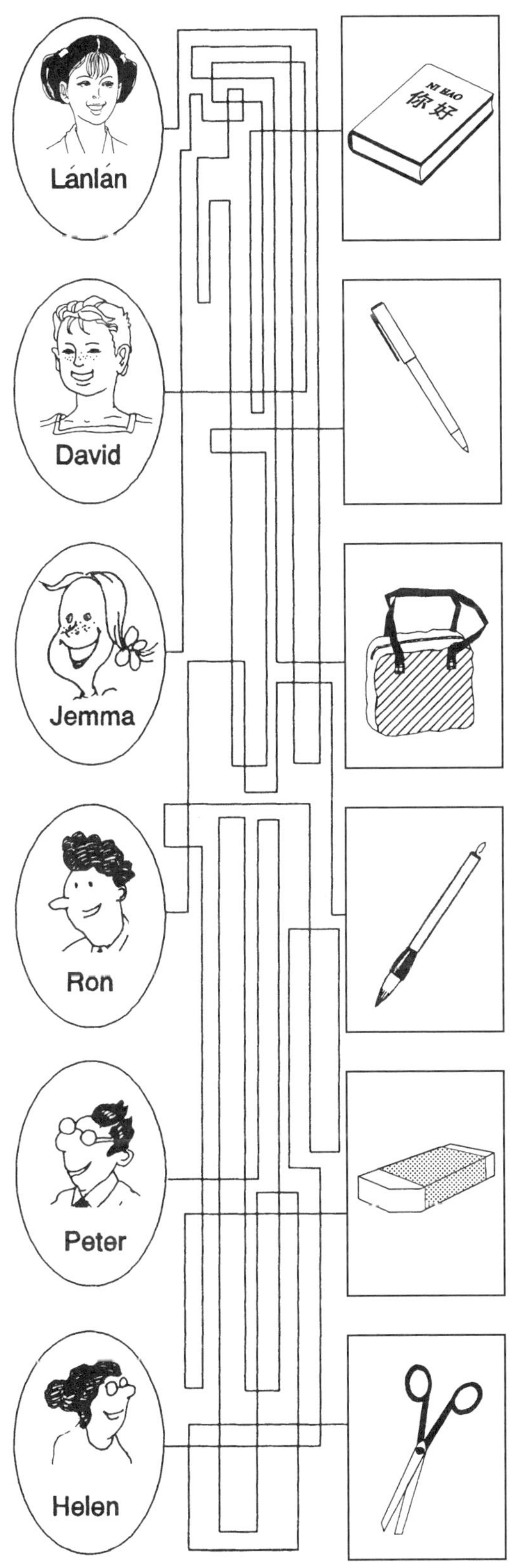

1. 這是大偉(Dàwěi)的書(shū)。

2. 這是 ______ 的 ______ 。

3. 這是 ______ 的 ______ 。

4. 這是 ______________ 。

5. ______________ 。

6. ______________ 。

E John was asked by the teacher to return some property. He mutters to himself while looking through the items. Find out what he is muttering about and answer the questions.

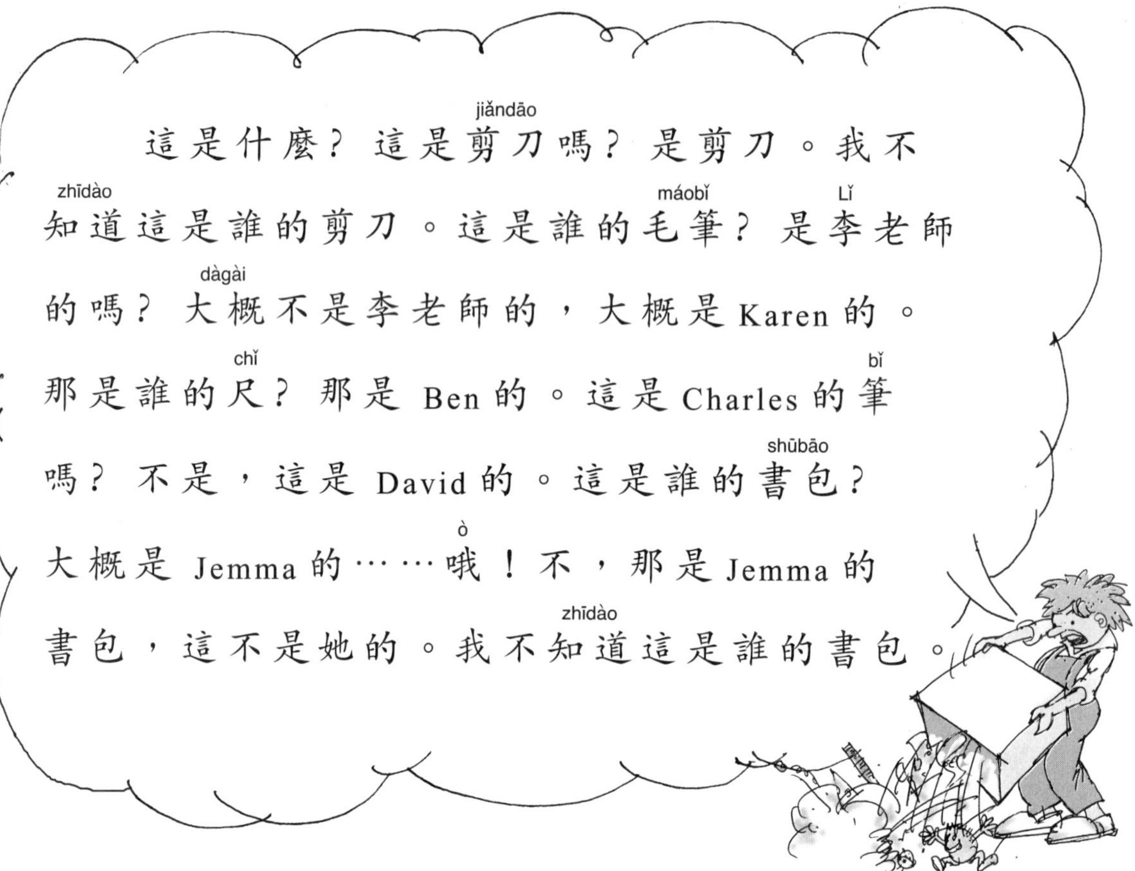

1. How many items did John look through? What are they?

2. List the items for which John knows the owner and indicate who they belong to.

3. List the items for which John does not know the owner.

F How do you say the following in Chinese? Tell the class first, then write your answers.

1. What is this? ______________________________

2. Whose is that? ______________________________

3. That is mine. ______________________________

4. Do you know? ______________________________

5. I know. ______________________________

6. I don’t know. ______________________________

7. Is this yours? ______________________________

8. This is not yours. ______________________________

9. Thank you. ______________________________

10. You are welcome. ______________________________

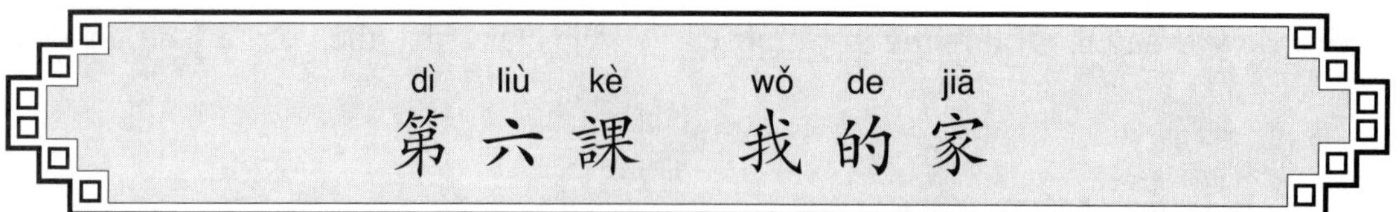

A Can you recognize these characters? Color each character according to the color indicated. The numbers in each character indicate the stroke order.

一 - red　二 - orange　三 - yellow　四 - green　五 - blue
六 - pink　七 - purple　八 - brown　九 - white　十 - grey
十一 - light blue　十二 - light green　十三 - black

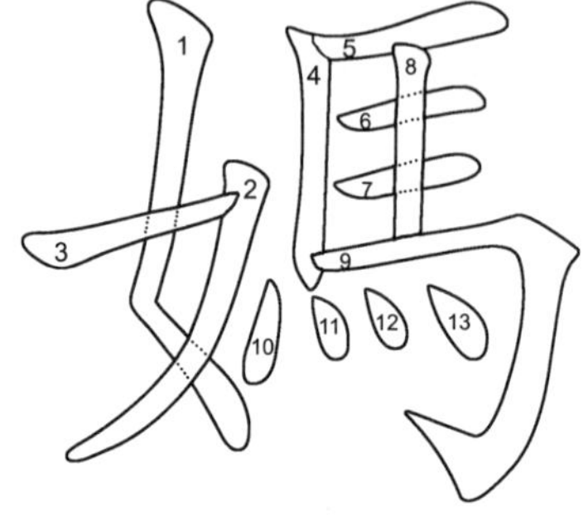

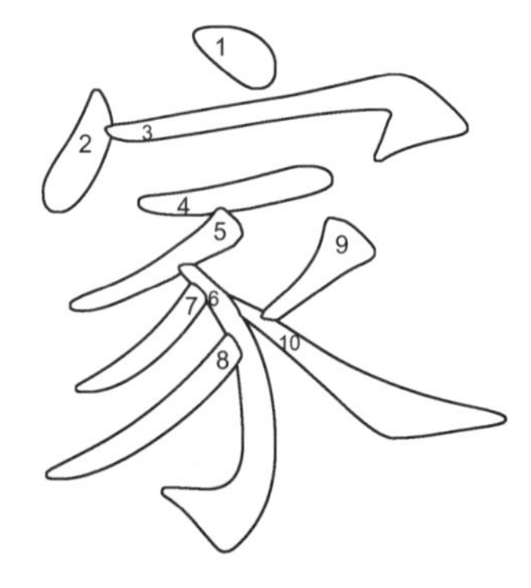

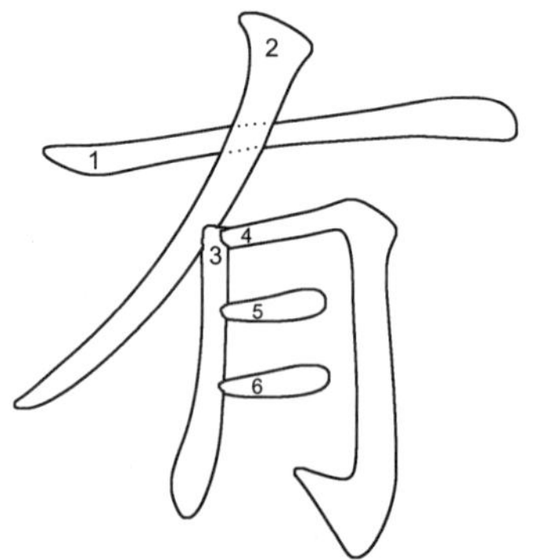

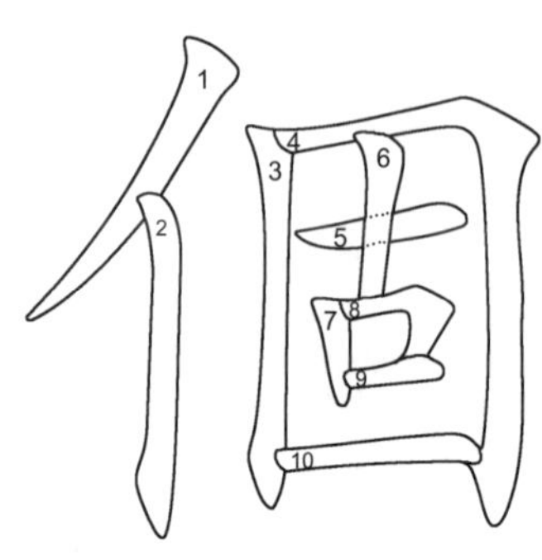

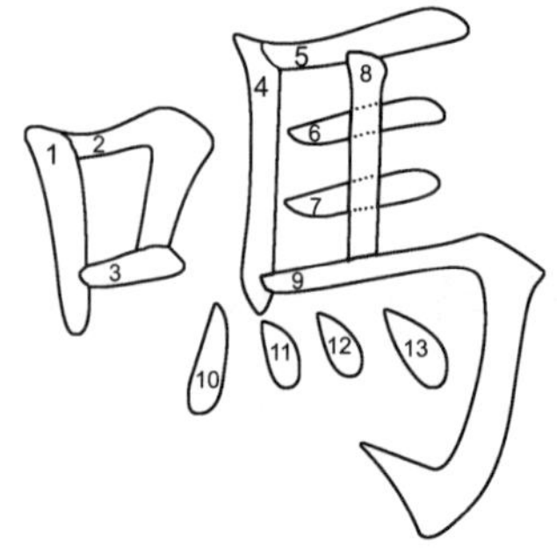

B This is your family tree. Draw pictures (or paste photographs) of your family members in the ovals. For each member, write the form of address on the first line and their age on the second line. You will use this to introduce your family to the class.

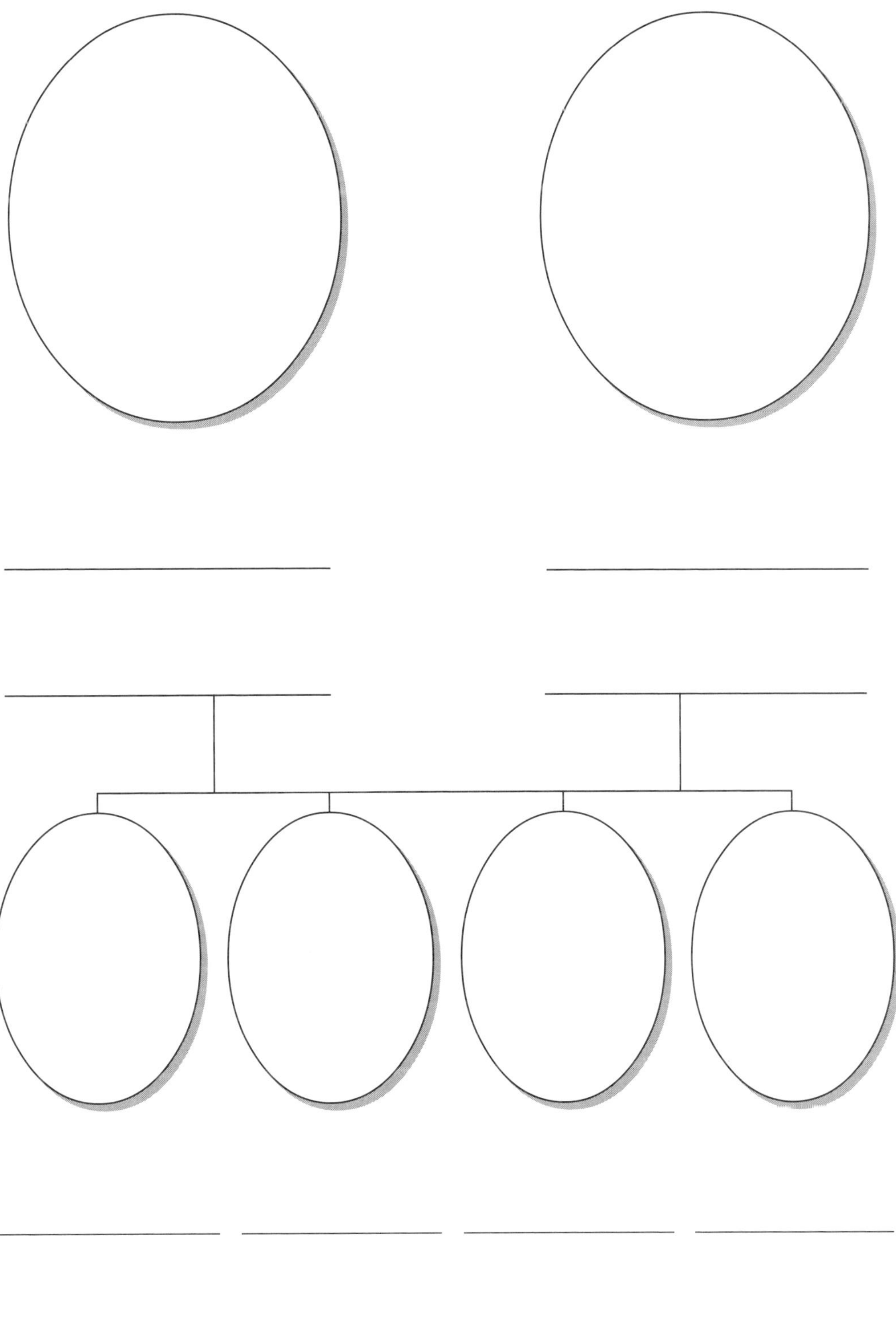

C These people are telling each other about how many people there are in their family. Help them to complete the conversation.

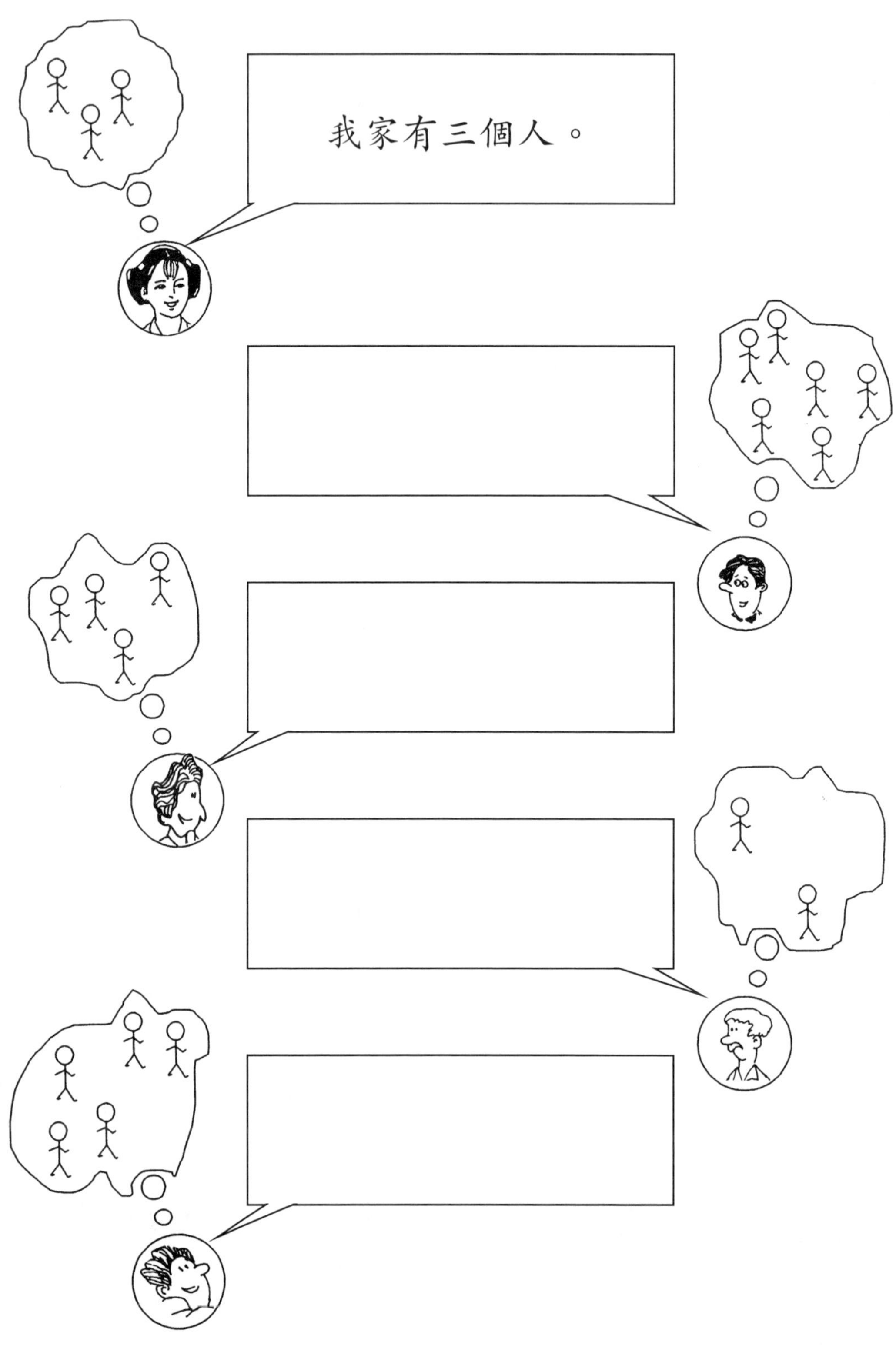

D Describe the siblings for each of the following.

1. 

2. 

3. Karen

4. 

5. Ben

6. 

7. 

E 蘭蘭 Lánlán is conducting a survey and asking you questions about your family. Answer each of her questions.

1. 你家有幾個人?

____

2. 你有哥哥嗎?

____

3. 你有弟弟嗎?

____

4. 你有幾個妹妹?

____

5. 你有幾個姊姊?

____

6. 你媽媽是老師嗎?

____

F Write the pinyin of each word/phrase listed below, then find and circle it in the word puzzle.

B	A	M	H	U	M	A	M	U	A	H	U	B	A
S	I	X	U	E	S	H	E	N	G	L	E	S	H
I	S	I	S	I	X	T	I	L	G	B	A	M	A
G	T	W	H	T	W	T	M	E	I	Y	O	U	R
E	I	E	I	E	I	I	E	I	E	E	I	E	I
J	I	S	T	D	I	J	I	E	J	I	E	N	T
J	A	I	J	I	A	N	G	E	G	G	S	I	X
A	I	J	I	D	I	D	D	Y	O	O	R	R	Y
N	I	J	J	I	N	N	I	A	N	I	A	N	I
A	N	G	Y	I	S	H	E	N	G	G	S	S	R
F	R	O	M	M	O	U	T	H	R	A	N	C	H
A	B	A	B	A	B	G	G	G	E	G	E	R	E
F	R	O	M	M	O	U	T	H	N	U	R	S	E
O	L	D	L	A	O	S	H	I	R	T	S	I	T

1. father ________________
2. mother ________________
3. elder brother ________________
4. younger brother ________________
5. elder sister ________________
6. younger sister ________________
7. laborer ________________
8. nurse ________________
9. doctor ________________
10. teacher ________________
11. student ________________
12. this year ________________
13. do/does not have ________________
14. family ________________

G These people are showing their family photos. Help them to complete their introduction.

Age: 34　　Age: 29

這是我的 ________________ 。

他今年 ________________ 。

他是 ________________ 。

Age: 35　　Age: 11

________________________________ 。

________________________________ 。

________________________________ 。

Age: 72　　Age: 80

________________________________ 。

________________________________ 。

________________________________ 。

Age: 40　　Age: 18

________________________________ 。

________________________________ 。

________________________________ 。

H You are conducting a survey about family members. Write five questions you need for this survey. Then ask your friends the questions to complete the table below.

1. ______________________________

2. ______________________________

3. ______________________________

4. ______________________________

5. ______________________________

Name	Number of family members	Number of elder brothers	Number of elder sisters	Number of younger brothers	Number of younger sisters
Average					

I This is the first letter you received from your pen pal in China. Read his letter and answer the questions.

XX: 你好！

我叫 (jiào) 林 (Lín) 六，今年 (jīnnián) 十五歲，是學生。我爸爸今年三十七歲，他是老師。我媽媽四十九歲，她是工人 (gōngrén)。我有兩個哥哥，三個姊姊，我沒 (méi) 有弟弟、妹妹。

林六

1. Give personal details of your pen pal.

2. How many people are there in his family?

3. What are his parents' ages and occupations?

4. How is his family structure different from the norm in China today?

J Use the form below to tell your Chinese pen pal about your family. Include the number of family members, their names, ages and occupations.

______________ :

____

____

____

____

____

____

____

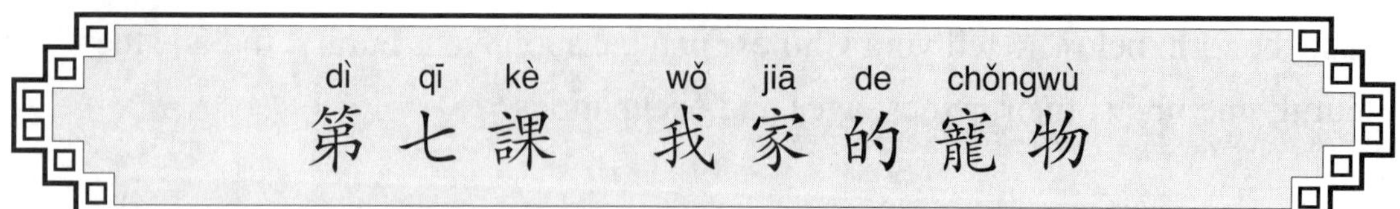

dì qī kè　wǒ jiā de chǒngwù
第七課　我家的寵物

A Choose the correct answer for each drawing.

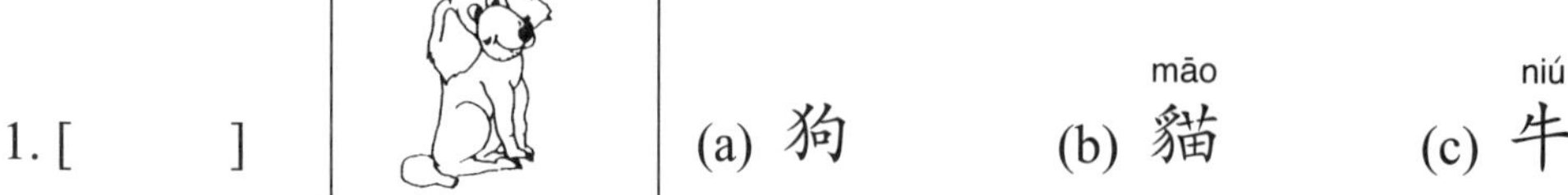

1. [　　　] (a) 狗　(b) 貓 (māo)　(c) 牛 (niú)

2. [　　　] (a) 貓　(b) 金魚 (jīnyú)　(c) 馬

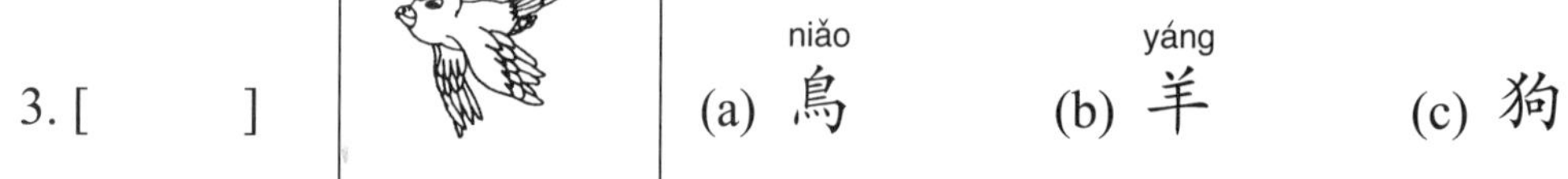

3. [　　　] (a) 鳥 (niǎo)　(b) 羊 (yáng)　(c) 狗

4. [　　　] (a) 兔 (tù)　(b) 金魚　(c) 龍 (lóng)

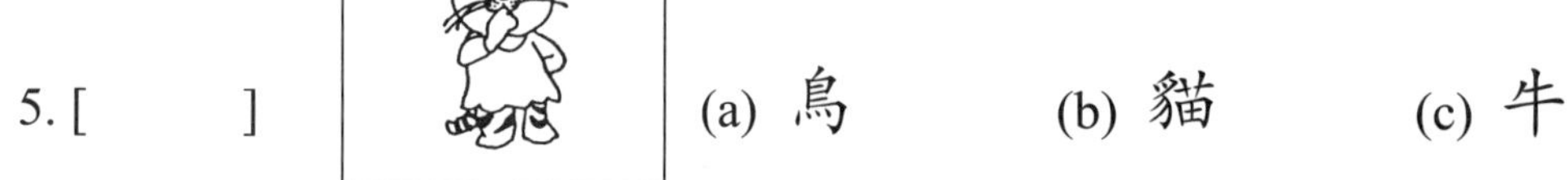

5. [　　　] (a) 鳥　(b) 貓　(c) 牛

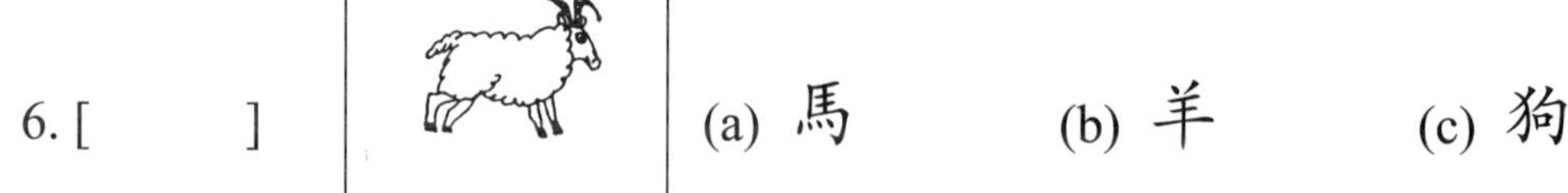

6. [　　　] (a) 馬　(b) 羊　(c) 狗

7. [　　　] (a) 龍　(b) 鳥　(c) 鼠 (shǔ)

B Listen to the tape and choose the correct answer.

1. [ ] a. I have three dogs.
   b. I have three cats.
   c. I have three birds.

2. [ ] a. Susan has five birds.
   b. Susan has five goldfish.
   c. Susan has five horses.

3. [ ] a. Peter has three cats.
   b. Peter has five cats.
   c. Peter has one cat.

4. [ ] a. Jemma has ten birds.
   b. Jemma has four cats.
   c. Jemma has fourteen birds.

5. [ ] a. Paul has eight horses.
   b. Paul has three dogs.
   c. Paul has five goldfish.

C Tell the class the number of pets you have at home and record the number of pets each classmate has.

Name						Other
(you)						
Average						

D Roger owns a small farm. Help him count his animals.

我是 Roger。我家有

1. ________ 匹 (pī) ________ ，

2. ________ 隻 ________ ，

3. ________ ______ ________ ，

4. ________ ______ ________ ，

5. ________ ______ ________ 。

E Listen to the description on the tape and write correct (✓) or incorrect (✗) in each space.

1. [   ] My dog is very fierce.
2. [   ] My horse is very small.
3. [   ] My goldfish are very cute.
4. [   ] I have a cat and he is very cute.
5. [   ] I have a bird and he is very big and aggressive.

F Choose from 很大，很小，很凶 (xiōng)，很可愛 (kě'ài) to describe the cartoon figure in each picture.

1 

2 

3 

______ ______ ______

4 

5 

6 

______ ______ ______

7 

8 

9 

______ ______ ______

G You found this column in a personal profile section in a Chinese children's magazine. Read the person's profile and answer the questions.

我叫(jiào)林(Lín)家師，今年十三歲，是學生(xuéshēng)。我爸爸四十七歲，是醫生(yīshēng)；媽媽三十五歲，是護士(hùshì)。我沒有哥哥、姊姊，也(yě)沒有弟弟、妹妹。我的寵物是貓(māo)和(hé)金魚(jīnyú)。我有兩隻貓；牠(tā)們很小，很可愛(kě'ài)。我有十條(tiáo)金魚，兩條很大，八條很小；牠(tā)們都很凶(xiōng)。

1. What is the writer's name and age?

2. What are his parents' occupations?

3. How many members does he have in his family?

4. What pets does he have? Describe them in detail.

H These are questions about pets. Write your answers on the lines below.

1. 你家有什麼寵物?

____

2. 你家有沒有馬?

____

3. 你家有幾隻狗?

____

4. 這隻貓(māo)是誰的?

Mary's

____

5. Peter 家有幾條(tiáo)金魚(jīnyú)?

Peter's

____

6. 他家有什麼寵物?

____

I Make a poster about your family, including your pets. You may draw pictures or paste small photos.

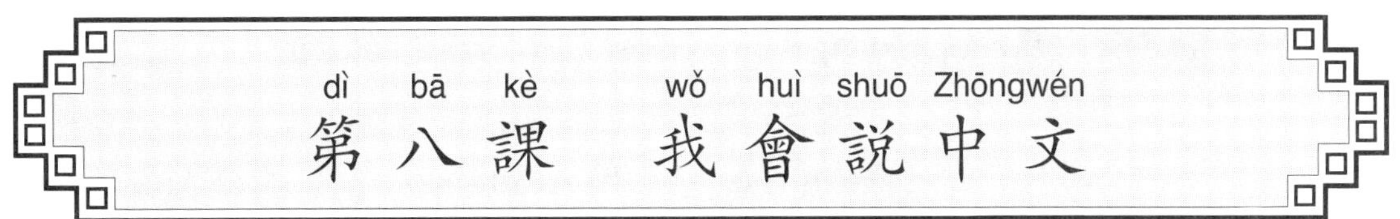

dì bā kè wǒ huì shuō Zhōngwén
第八課　我會說中文

A These people are from various countries. Answer the questions.

1. Q: 大明 (Dàmíng) 是哪 (nǎ) 國人？

   A: ______________________

2. Q: Marie 是哪國人？

   A: ______________________

3. Q: Peter 是哪國人？

   A: ______________________

4. Q: 大偉 (Dàwěi) 是哪國人？

   A: ______________________

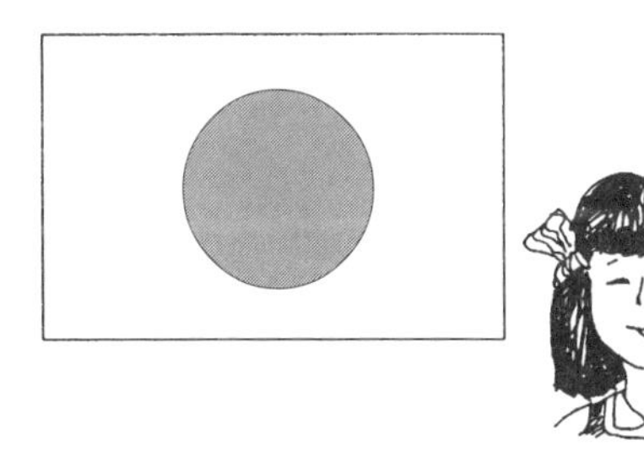

5. Q: Anna 是哪國人？

   A: ______________________

6. Q: Yumi 是哪國人？

   A: ______________________

B Listen to the description on the tape and choose the correct answer.

1. [ ]	Mary is	(a) Chinese	(b) Australian	(c) American
2. [ ]	David is	(a) Australian	(b) German	(c) Japanese
3. [ ]	Helen is	(a) British	(b) a New Zealander	(c) Australian
4. [ ]	Keiko is	(a) Canadian	(b) Japanese	(c) German
5. [ ]	Sylvia is	(a) American	(b) Australian	(c) German

C Fill in your ID card in English.

Name: ________________

Age: ________________

Nationality:

____

Use the information on your ID card to write, in Chinese, three sentences to introduce yourself to the class.

1. ______________________________

2. ______________________________

3. ______________________________

D Help these three people to introduce themselves.

jiào
你好。我叫 ______________ 。

jīnnián
我今年 ___________ 歲。

我是 ____________________ 。

hé Zhōngwén
我會說 _________ 和中文。

Chris, 8
American
speaks English
& Chinese

你好。我叫 _____________ 。

jīnnián
我今年 _____________ 。

我是 ____________________ 。

hé
我會說 _______ 和 _______ 。

Don, 92
German
speaks German
& Chinese

_________ 。__________ Keiko。

我今年 _____________ 。

我是 ____________________ 。

我會說 _______ 和 _______ 。

Keiko, 9
Japanese
speaks Japanese
& Chinese

E Write the Pinyin of each word/phrase listed below, then find and circle it in the word puzzle.

```
R A N N I N G U O R E N I N
F O U M E I G U O R E N N I
I D I D N O F O U I X Z Z N
H A N Y U U F O U Y I H H R
L L L Y J I A N A D A E O R
X I X I N A G U O R E N N M
I Y I N G G U O R I Q G G E
Y A N G U O O R I B I U G I
I R A Y E S S I R E N O U G
D E G U O O H O M N G R O U
I N A G A R U N G E W E R A
A U S T Z H O N G W E N E N
N O I X I N X I L A N I N X
R E B E E D I D U I B U Q I
```

1. Chinese ________________
2. American ________________
3. England ________________
4. Germany ________________
5. Canada ________________
6. New Zealand ________________
7. Japan ________________
8. Australian ________________
9. excuse me ________________
10. may I ask you ________________
11. what nationality ________________
12. Chinese language ________________
13. a little ________________
14. that's all right ________________

F These three people have become good friends although they are from different cultural backgrounds. Read their personal profiles and answer the questions.

jiào Xiǎoyǎ Rìběnrén
她叫山口小亞，是日本人。她的寵物是一隻大狗。山口小亞有兩個哥哥，一個弟弟。
Yīngyǔ de Rìyǔ
她英語說得很好，日語說得不好。

jiào Bái Mǎlì
她叫白馬利，今年十九歲。她爸爸是中國人，媽媽是日本人。白馬利沒有寵物。她有四個妹妹，兩個弟弟。她英語說得很好，也會
yìdiǎn Zhōngwén hé
說一點中文和一點日語。

Jiělì
她叫李姊利，是中國人，今年十五歲。
Àozhōurén
她爸爸是中國人，媽媽是澳洲人。李姊利
dōu
英語和中文都說得很好。她有一個哥哥。她哥哥英語說得很好，中文說得不好。

1. Who can speak Chinese? How well does each speak?

2. Who can speak English? How well does each speak?

3. Who is from the largest family? What siblings does she have?

G When you visit China, you will often hear people say the following to you. Write your response in each situation.

1. 請問 (qǐngwèn)，你是哪 (nǎ) 國人？

____

2. 你會不會說中文 (Zhōngwén)？

____

3. 你是美國人 (Měiguórén) 嗎？

____

4. 你是不是加拿大人 (Jiānádàrén)？

____

5. 對不起 (duìbùqǐ)。

____

6. 你說得 (de) 很好。

____

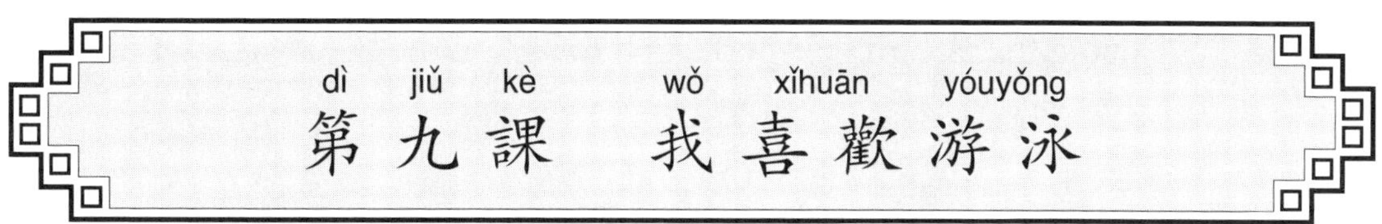

A Listen to the tape and choose the correct answer.

1. [ ]  a.  b.  c. 

2. [ ] a.  b.  c. 

3. [ ] a.  b.  c. 

4. [ ] a.  b.  c. 

5. [ ] a.  b.  c. 

6. [ ] a.  b.  c. 

B Choose the Chinese for each of the sports pictured and write the answer on the line.

1.  騎車（qíchē），跑步（pǎobù），打乒乓球（pīngpāngqiú） ____________

2.  打網球（wǎngqiú），游泳（yóuyǒng），踢足球（tī zúqiú） ____________

3.  騎車，打乒乓球，跑步 ____________

4.  打籃球（lánqiú），打網球，游泳 ____________

5.  踢足球，游泳，打棒球（bàngqiú） ____________

6. 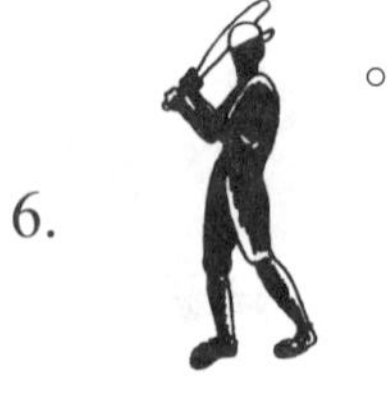 打棒球，打網球，跑步 ____________

7.  打棒球，游泳，打網球 ____________

C These people like one sport better than another. Listen to the tape and number each sport from 1 to 4 according to his/her preference.

_______ _______ _______ _______

_______ _______ _______ _______

_______ _______ _______ _______

D Write the Pinyin of each word/phrase listed below, then find and circle it in the word puzzle.

A	D	D	T	I	M	E	S	T	W	O	H	E	R
D	D	A	W	A	N	G	Q	I	U	D	A	D	A
A	A	L	L	B	B	B	F	R	O	M	D	A	D
A	L	A	L	U	M	I	N	I	M	B	E	P	P
N	X	N	N	X	I	W	A	T	A	M	E	I	S
S	W	Q	I	I	C	H	Y	U	N	D	O	N	G
Q	Q	I	C	H	E	E	Q	I	G	C	C	G	H
U	B	U	Q	U	M	B	R	E	L	L	A	P	S
A	D	A	D	A	B	A	N	G	Q	I	U	A	S
A	N	I	M	N	O	T	E	A	S	Y	I	N	O
H	E	L	L	O	Y	Y	O	U	Y	O	N	G	S
N	O	T	M	A	N	Y	D	U	I	B	U	Q	I
T	H	I	S	I	S	I	T	I	Z	U	Q	I	U
P	A	U	L	J	E	M	S	P	A	O	B	U	S

1. play tennis ________________
2. play basketball ________________
3. cycling ________________
4. play baseball ________________
5. play table tennis ________________
6. play soccer ________________
7. jogging ________________
8. swimming ________________
9. sports ________________
10. busy ________________
11. do not like ________________
12. sorry ________________
13. not going ________________

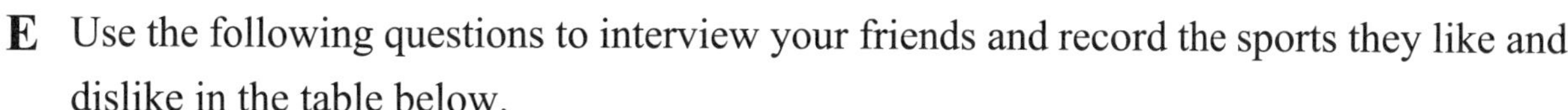

E Use the following questions to interview your friends and record the sports they like and dislike in the table below.

Q1: 你最(zuì)喜歡什麼運動?

Q2: 你最不喜歡什麼運動?

Names	likes	dislikes

According to the results of your survey, answer the following questions in Chinese.

1. What's the most popular sport?

____

2. What's the least popular sport?

____

F Listen to the tape and draw a line connecting the person to the sport he/she likes.

Ron

Tom

David

Jenny

Chris

Jim

G Use the information in Exercise **F** to answer the following questions.

1. Tom 喜歡什麼運動?

____

2. Chris 喜歡什麼運動?

____

3. Ron 喜歡游泳(yóuyǒng)嗎？

____

4. 誰喜歡踢(tī)足球(zúqiú)？

____

5. 誰喜歡騎車(qíchē)？

____

6. 誰喜歡打網球(wǎngqiú)？

____

H Here are some squares for you to play bingo or tick-tack-toe.

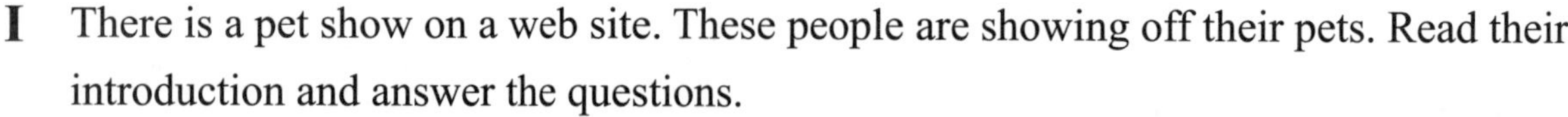

I There is a pet show on a web site. These people are showing off their pets. Read their introduction and answer the questions.

THE PET SHOW

- 我的狗叫(jiào)山山。牠(tā)五歲，不凶(xiōng)。山山喜歡騎車(qíchē)、跑步(pǎobù)和(hé)游泳(yóuyǒng)。牠會打籃球(lánqiú)和踢(tī)足球(zúqiú)。
- 我的小鳥(niǎo)叫加加(Jiājiā)。牠四歲。加加喜歡打乒乓球(pīngpāngqiú)，不喜歡游泳。牠會說中文(Zhōngwén)、英語(Yīngyǔ)和日語(Rìyǔ)。牠最喜歡說「我不去。」
- 我的貓(māo)叫毛毛(Máomao)。牠六歲。牠喜歡打網球(wǎngqiú)、打籃球和踢足球。毛毛不喜歡游泳。

1. Based on the information given, which one do you think is the most active? Give reasons.

2. Which one is the least active? Give reasons.

3. Which one would you vote for and why?

You have a pet to enter this show. Draw your pet and write an introduction.

____

____

____

____

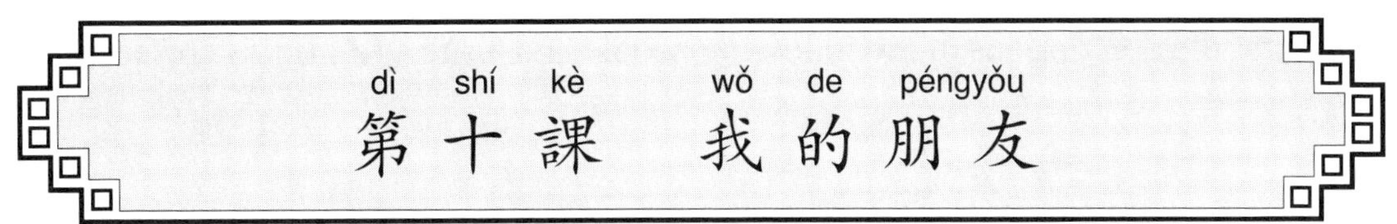

第十課　我的朋友

dì shí kè　wǒ de péngyǒu

A This is a picture of 蘭蘭 Lánlán's friend. Label the parts of her head.

B Who is Jason's friend? Circle the correct answer.

你好。我是 Jason　。我的朋友眼睛(yǎnjīng)很大，頭髮(tóufǎ)很長。她的鼻子(bízi)很大，嘴巴(zuǐbā)很小。

C Listen to the descriptions of the following people and write a (✓) if it is correct or a (✗) if not.

D Draw a picture of a famous person who has a distinctive feature. Write a description in Chinese then read it aloud for your class to guess who the person is.

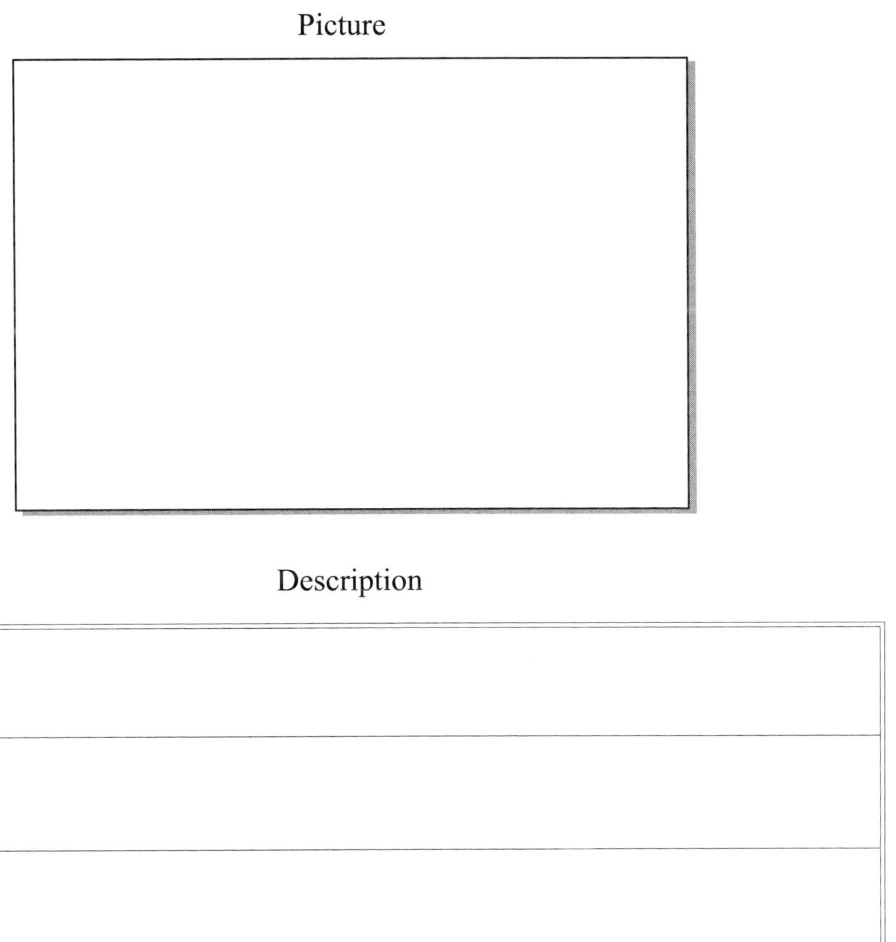

Description

E Draw pictures of the people your classmates describe and try to guess who they are.

F Make an identity card for the missing person described below.

Wáng Dàzhōng　jīnnián

他叫王大中，今年十一歲，上五年級。他是

Yīngyǔ　liǎn　cháng　tóufǎ　duǎn

中國人，會說英語。他的臉很長，頭髮很短，

bízi　zuǐbā　yǎnjīng　méimáo

鼻子很大，嘴巴很小。他的眼睛很小，眉毛

很長。

Information	Descriptions
Name: ______	Face: ______
Nationality: ______	Hair: ______
Age: ______	Eyes: ______
Grade: ______	Eyebrows: ______
Language spoken: ______	Nose: ______
	Mouth: ______

G Write in Chinese what you should say in the following situations.

1. You would like to invite a friend to go swimming.

____

2. You accept your friend's invitation to play tennis.

____

3. As you don't like playing baseball you decline your friend's invitation.

____

4. How do you say that you are in grade seven at school?

____

5. How do you say that you and Robert are in the same class?

____

6. How do you say "Let's go!"?

____

H You are entering a competition to create an alien. Draw your alien and give his/her facial description.

(My alien)

____

____

____

____

____

____

In your group of four, each takes a turn to describe his/her alien for the others to draw. Then decide whose design is the most creative.

The winner:______________________________

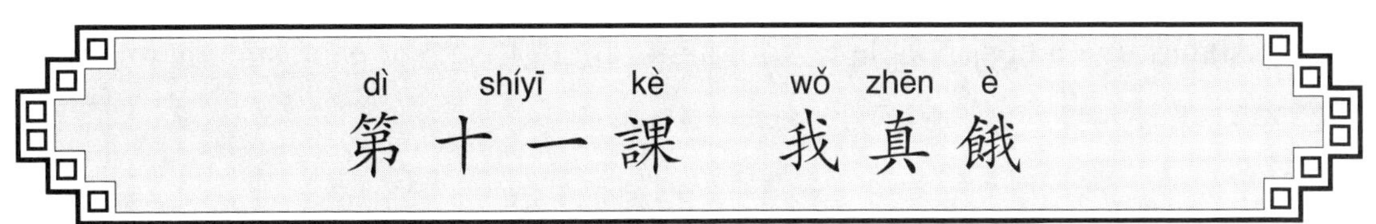

A Choose the correct answer for each drawing.

1. [　　　]  (a) 漢堡 (hànbǎo) (b) 三明治 (sānmíngzhì) (c) 春捲 (chūnjuǎn)

2. [　　　]  (a) 熱狗 (règǒu) (b) 冰淇淋 (bīngqílín) (c) 牛奶 (niúnǎi)

3. [　　　]  (a) 果汁 (guǒzhī) (b) 春捲 (c) 熱狗

4. [　　　] 

(a) 漢堡 (b) 冰淇淋 (c) 牛奶

5. [　　　]  (a) 三明治 (b) 炸蝦片 (zháxiāpiàn) (c) 炒飯 (chǎofàn)

6. [　　　]  (a) 牛奶 (b) 炒飯 (c) 春捲

7. [　　　]  (a) 三明治 (b) 漢堡 (c) 炒飯

8. [　　　]  (a) 冰淇淋 (b) 熱狗 (c) 果汁

9. [　　　]  (a) 炸蝦片 (b) 三明治 (c) 牛奶

B In a restaurant you hear people talking about food. Listen to each statement and choose the correct answer.

1. [ ] Emma likes to eat **(a)** sweet and sour pork **(b)** ice cream **(c)** sandwiches.

2. [ ] Anna likes to eat **(a)** hot dogs **(b)** fried rice **(c)** sandwiches.

3. [ ] Lanlan likes to eat **(a)** hot dogs **(b)** spring rolls **(c)** fried rice.

4. [ ] Mark likes to drink **(a)** milk **(b)** juice **(c)** water.

5. [ ] Clair likes **(a)** sandwiches **(b)** Chinese food **(c)** hamburgers.

6. [ ] Peter does not like **(a)** spring rolls **(b)** hamburgers **(c)** Chinese food.

7. [ ] Karen feels like having **(a)** juice **(b)** an ice cream **(c)** a sandwich.

8. [ ] Sally is **(a)** very hungry **(b)** not hungry **(c)** not well.

9. [ ] Charles is **(a)** not thirsty **(b)** very hungry **(c)** very thirsty.

10. [ ] Nicholas **(a)** can **(b)** cannot **(c)** likes to use chopsticks.

C Write the Pinyin of each word/phrase listed below, then find and circle it in the word puzzle.

Z	H	A	X	I	A	P	I	A	N	K	F	G	C
Z	Y	D	H	A	N	B	A	O	B	A	O	K	H
Z	D	R	E	D	D	C	N	N	I	U	N	A	I
H	A	M	B	A	O	H	I	A	N	Z	Y	X	F
O	N	E	D	I	H	U	N	M	F	I	G	S	A
N	I	N	G	M	E	N	G	J	I	P	I	A	N
G	L	U	U	U	N	J	E	K	C	Y	Z	N	A
G	F	Y	L	E	K	U	G	J	H	Z	R	M	T
U	Y	E	U	Y	E	A	K	U	A	I	Z	I	E
O	E	Y	R	E	L	N	G	G	O	L	D	N	T
C	O	L	K	N	E	O	N	S	F	O	G	G	S
A	F	G	U	O	Z	H	I	E	A	T	E	Z	I
I	B	I	N	G	Q	I	L	I	N	O	U	H	N
F	G	U	L	A	O	R	O	U	E	S	H	I	H

1. lemon chicken ______________

2. prawn crackers ______________

3. sweet & sour pork ______________

4. spring rolls ______________

5. juice ______________

6. sandwich ______________

7. hamburger ______________

8. milk ______________

9. ice cream ______________

10. fried rice ______________

11. to have a meal ______________

12. very thirsty ______________

13. chopsticks ______________

14. Chinese food ______________

D You are to prepare lunch and dinner. Write your menu in Chinese.

Lunch

Dinner

E A bachelor is looking for a Chinese girlfriend. This is his description of himself.

你好！我叫 Blair，今年(jīnnián)三十九歲，是美國人(Měiguórén)，會說一點(yìdiǎn)中文(Zhōngwén)。我喜歡運動。游泳(yóuyǒng)、騎車(qíchē)、跑步(pǎobù)，我都(dōu)喜歡。我最(zuì)喜歡的是打棒球(bàngqiú)和踢(tī)足球(zúqiú)。我也喜歡騎馬(qímǎ)。我的寵物是兩匹(pī)小馬。我會做(zuò)中國菜，會拿(ná)筷子(kuàizi)。我最喜歡的中國菜是炒飯(chǎofàn)和咕咾肉(gūlǎoròu)。

1. What is his age and nationality?

2. Is he an active person? Give detailed evidence to support your answer.

3. What contact does he have with Chinese culture? List the details.

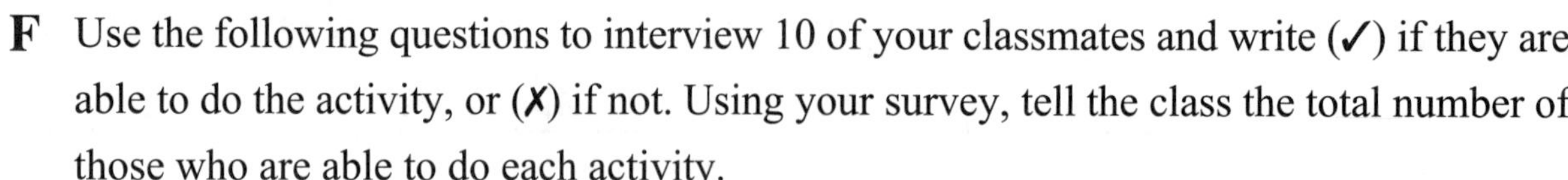

F Use the following questions to interview 10 of your classmates and write (✓) if they are able to do the activity, or (✗) if not. Using your survey, tell the class the total number of those who are able to do each activity.

huì búhuì ná kuàizi
1. 你會不會拿筷子？

zuò
2. 你會不會做中國菜？

Zhōngwén
3. 你會不會說中文？

pīngpāngqiú
4. 你會不會打乒乓球？

Name				
幾個人？				

A Paul has received a letter from his pen pal in China. Listen while the letter is being read and then answer the following questions.

1. How old is she?

   ____

2. In which grade is she at school?

   ____

3. How many people are there in her family?

   ____

4. What is her mother's occupation?

   ____

5. How old is her younger brother?

   ____

6. Does her younger brother like ice cream?

   ____

7. What does she like to eat?

   ____

B Jack has extracted a few sentences from a letter written by his Chinese pen pal. Jack has just started to study Chinese and has rewritten them in the wrong order. Help him to rearrange the order in each sentence and write the meaning.

1. 人是我國中。

   Chinese: ______________________________

   Meaning: ______________________________

2. 六級上年我。

   Chinese: ______________________________

   Meaning: ______________________________

3. 嗎國是美你人?

   Chinese: ______________________________

   Meaning: ______________________________

4. 人家有個我三。

   Chinese: ______________________________

   Meaning: ______________________________

5. 國你中喜菜嗎歡?

   Chinese: ______________________________

   Meaning: ______________________________

C In a magazine column, these people are looking for pen pals. Read their profiles and answer the questions.

> 林(Lín)國喜　二十五歲；會說一點(yìdiǎn)英語(Yīngyǔ)；沒有寵物；喜歡打籃球(lánqiú)和乒乓球(pīngpāngqiú)；不喜歡吃三明治(sānmíngzhì)和漢堡(hànbǎo)。

> 馬家歡　十五歲；英語說得(de)很好，也會說一點日語(Rìyǔ)；喜歡寵物，有兩隻狗；喜歡打網球(wǎngqiú)和游泳(yóuyǒng)，不喜歡踢(tī)足球(zúqiú)；最(zuì)喜歡吃的中國菜是咕咾肉(gūlǎoròu)。

> 白(Bái)亞中(Yǎzhōng)　十二歲；日語說得很好，英語說得不好；有三隻貓；不喜歡運動；喜歡吃炸蝦片(zháxiāpiàn)和漢堡。

> 李(Lǐ)喜蘭(Xǐlán)　十三歲；英語說得很好，會說一點德語(Déyǔ)；不喜歡寵物；喜歡運動，最喜歡打網球(wǎngqiú)和踢(tī)足球(zúqiú)。

1. If you are choosing a pen pal from these four, which one would you choose and why?

2. Which one would you definitely not choose and why?

3. Choose one for a friend of yours and explain your reasons.

D Introduce yourself in a letter to your pen pal in China. Include your age, family, nationalities, pets, likes and dislikes. Use as many characters as you can.

______________：

E Write in Chinese what you should say in the following situations.

1. When someone does you a favor.

   ____

2. When your guest arrives.

   ____

3. When you accidentally step on someone's foot.

   ____

4. When someone thanks you for lending him/her a dictionary.

   ____

5. When someone says that you speak Chinese well.

   ____

6. When someone apologizes for being late.

   ____

7. When you ask someone for information.

   ____

F On some occasions you may see some signs in Chinese. For each of the signs pictured below, write the Pinyin on the first line and the meaning on the next line.

Writing exercise

How to write a character correctly:

1. Write the strokes according to the numbered sequence.
2. Start each stroke beginning where the number is located.
3. End a stroke with the pen lifted off the paper if it has a pointy end, or with the pen stopped on the paper if it has a round end.

Trace the two lightly printed examples and maintain the proportions in the practice boxes.
The first space is for you to write the Pinyin and meaning of each character.

	Character	Pinyin / Meaning	Trace	Trace
1	人	*Pinyin:* *Meaning:*	人	人
	山	*P:* *M:*	山	山
	口	*P:* *M:*	口	口
2	你	*P:* *M:*	你	你
	好	*P:* *M:*	好	好
	我	*P:* *M:*	我	我
	是	*P:* *M:*	是	是

他	P: M:	他 他
們	P: M:	們 們
3 一	P: M:	一 一
二	P: M:	二 二
三	P: M:	三 三
四	P: M:	四 四
五	P: M:	五 五
六	P: M:	六 六
七	P: M:	七 七

4

Character			
八	P: M:	八	八
九	P: M:	九	九
十	P: M:	十	十
誰	P: M:	誰	誰
她	P: M:	她	她
老	P: M:	老	老
師	P: M:	師	師
幾	P: M:	幾	幾
歲	P: M:	歲	歲

	Character			
	兩	*P:* *M:*	兩	兩
5	這	*P:* *M:*	這	這
	那	*P:* *M:*	那	那
	什	*P:* *M:*	什	什
	麼	*P:* *M:*	麼	麼
	嗎	*P:* *M:*	嗎	嗎
	的	*P:* *M:*	的	的
	不	*P:* *M:*	不	不
6	家	*P:* *M:*	家	家

字			
有	P: M:	有	有
個	P: M:	個	個
爸	P: M:	爸	爸
媽	P: M:	媽	媽
哥	P: M:	哥	哥
姊	P: M:	姊	姊
弟	P: M:	弟	弟
妹	P: M:	妹	妹
7 寵	P: M:	寵	寵

Character			
物	P: M:	物	物
隻	P: M:	隻	隻
狗	P: M:	狗	狗
馬	P: M:	馬	馬
很	P: M:	很	很
大	P: M:	大	大
小	P: M:	小	小
沒	P: M:	沒	沒
中	P: M:	中	中

Character	Pinyin / Meaning	Trace
國	P: M:	國 國
美	P: M:	美 美
加	P: M:	加 加
拿	P: M:	拿 拿
也	P: M:	也 也
會	P: M:	會 會
説	P: M:	説 説
9 喜	P: M:	喜 喜
歡	P: M:	歡 歡

運	P: M:									
	運	運								
動	P: M:									
	動	動								
打	P: M:									
	打	打								
球	P: M:									
	球	球								
去	P: M:									
	去	去								
吧	P: M:									
	吧	吧								
朋	P: M:									
	朋	朋								
友	P: M:									
	友	友								
叫	P: M:									
	叫	叫								

Character	Pinyin / Meaning	Tracing	Tracing
上	*P:* *M:*	上	上
年	*P:* *M:*	年	年
級	*P:* *M:*	級	級
和	*P:* *M:*	和	和
同	*P:* *M:*	同	同
學	*P:* *M:*	學	學
真	*P:* *M:*	真	真
餓	*P:* *M:*	餓	餓
吃	*P:* *M:*	吃	吃

11

想	P: M:								
	想	想							
渴	P: M:								
	渴	渴							
喝	P: M:								
	喝	喝							
菜	P: M:								
	菜	菜							
飯	P: M:								
	飯	飯							

For extra character practice:

Character Bricks

This picture of the Great Wall of China is made of bricks with all the Chinese chararcters you should learn to write in this book. Each time you learn a new character find it on the wall and color it in.